The Wonderful World of Transportation

On the way to the moon: Apollo 8 *leaves the launching pad, December 1968.*

The Wonderful World of Transportation

Laurie Lee
and David Lambert

Doubleday and Company Inc.

Garden City, New York

Contents

Certain words and phrases in this book are followed by the symbol☞. Whenever you see this symbol it means that you can look up the word or phrase in the alphabetical glossary at the end of the book and find more information or a fuller definition of the term.

1   Man Must Move

The story of transport began when man's ape-like ancestors descended from the trees and took their first upright steps on the ground. There is nothing motionless in the universe. The earth itself is in constant motion. It spins, revolves around the sun and, with its family of planets in the Milky Way, journeys millions of miles through space.

Man is also a wanderer, and has been since his beginnings. There is a natural instinct in most living things to escape from their birthplace, and to spread out. Only thus can they find space to breed.

Since man first appeared, about a quarter of a million years ago, he has spread wider than any other species on earth. He has increased his speed from a four-miles-an-hour walk to many thousand miles an hour through space, his ability to move loads from a few pounds on his back to the oil tanker's 200,000 tons. How has he done it? By his brains and his hands and his genius for invention.

Why does man move? He has many reasons, all the reasons of life itself—hunting, fighting, trading, mating, visiting, or just adventure. As soon as a child can crawl, it tries to move away from its cradle. An instinct in all of us makes us want to search and discover the world.

Originally, no doubt, the reason was hunger. Early man had to eat what he could: roots, berries, plants, fruits, and animals, when he could catch them. Searching for these would force him to move. Easily caught animals would learn to shun men and move away to other pastures. To live, man would follow them. But only so many beasts could live off so much land. Only so many men could live off those beasts. The rest of them had to travel even farther.

In time, early man colonized the earth, moving first in families and later in tribes, searching always for food and space. Little by little he spread out across Asia, seeking the new lands before him, and crossed into America from Siberia to Alaska by land bridge or shallow sea. The strong drove the weak before them, down America, Africa, and the

Edward H. White makes his 21-minute space walk from Gemini 4 *(1965).*

Pacific islands, until the earliest wanderers were pushed to the edges of the world, to remote islands in the Southern Hemisphere, such as Tasmania and Tierra del Fuego.

Here and there people settled, grew food, and raised cattle; but man still had reasons to move. Where tribes were small, young men would no doubt leave home, as they do today, to seek wives and set up on their own. When a society prospered and grew rich in goods, it would send merchants to barter with people living nearby. So trade began; it is still the most important reason for transport.

Another reason, even older than trade, was man's instinct for war. Poorer tribes would often attack their wealthier neighbors and rob them. Nomads whose cattle had died in drought would raid the settled

A man can carry 100 lb. at a speed of 3 m.p.h. First animals, then mechanized transport (left) enabled him to carry far heavier loads far faster (right).

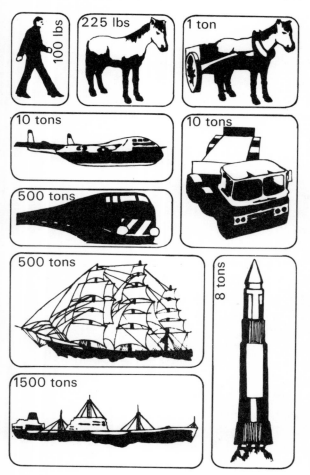

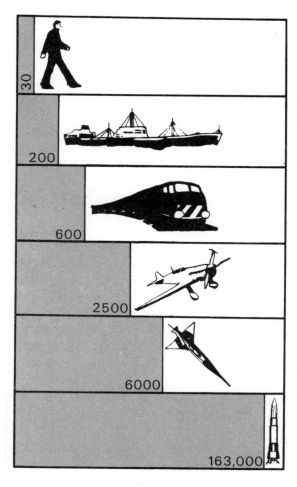

farmers for food. Expanding populations, throughout history, have invaded their neighbors' lands.

The first men to discover America were seeking food and somewhere to live. When Columbus rediscovered it, he was looking for spices, gold, and glory. It was also the spirit of adventure, the urge to be first on the scene, that made him face the terrors of the Atlantic; the same spirit has driven explorers to the poles and to the top of Everest.

Today millions of tourists travel about the world in search of its many marvels; they visit strange lands for no other reason than curiosity. Man is still, it seems, the most restless being on this restless sphere. He possesses an instinct enjoyed by few other animals—that is, to journey simply for pleasure.

An ancient wooden model from Egypt, showing a column of troops on the march. For centuries the speed of an army's advance was the speed of men on foot.

2 Man Travels Over Land

Man is a land animal. He takes naturally neither to air nor to water. In the dim past of prehistory, his ancestors used their hands and feet to move themselves about among the branches. When they descended to earth they found new uses for their adaptable limbs.

In the beginning, man was his own beast of burden; he carried loads on his back or dragged them along. As a transport animal, man is weak and slow, unable to travel much faster than four miles an hour. Yet the machinery that makes him walk is more wonderful than the most complex space rocket☞.

Each of us is built around a framework of bone, which keeps us from collapsing under the weight of our body tissues. This rigid skeleton is made up of many separate pieces, all neatly fitted into or against one another. Ball-and-socket joints at hip and shoulder allow us to move our limbs about.

Muscles, attached to our bones by tendons, are the springs and pistons of our movements. Nerves, like electric cables, carry messages to the "telephone exchanges" in our brain and spine. "Automatic operators," acting at about 150 miles an hour, flash back orders to our muscles, which obediently contract or relax. All this helps us keep our balance and tells us when and how to move. A child's first step is a miracle of coordination.

Most animals possess the machinery of movement. They use it in hunting, fighting, or wandering. They also use it to carry occasional light burdens—such as their newborn young, material for their homes, and food to eat or store. Early man moved for the same reasons and he carried the same simple burdens, but as his needs multiplied, man found reasons for carrying a greater variety of things.

In simple, primitive communities, everyone must have shared the daily tasks of carrying water, fuel, and food. Over long distances, people could carry weights only at walking pace. But no doubt messengers ran

An 1828 forecast of travel, in which steam locomotives reduce a city to chaos.

with news from one community to the next. Man had begun to transport objects and ideas.

How long was it before early man learned to use animals to help carry burdens? The taming of wild animals to provide labor and food was one of the first great steps in man's history, making it possible for him to travel longer distances and to move heavier loads. We do not know exactly when the idea began, but it is not difficult to guess how it happened.

The dog was almost certainly the first tame animal, and it is possible that he tamed himself. Wild dogs hunt in packs, and they are also scavengers. They must have watched early man hunting animals, as hyenas watch a lion attacking its prey. When man had killed and eaten his fill, the dogs would creep toward the carcass and help themselves. They would linger by man's camps, hoping for scraps of food; they would follow him when he went hunting and help him to trace the scent. So man and dog learned to live together, for each was useful to the other. Soon, with the aid of simple harness, the dog became a work animal as well as a hunting aid.

Next came the idea of using larger animals for heavier work, a much more important step. Primitive man was a hunter who used clumsy stone weapons, and of course he often went hungry. To assure himself of a store of meat, man learned to use dogs to help him round up wild animals. He kept the creatures in a stockade as a living larder.

The hunter had become a herdsman, raising captive cattle for food. But he still had to keep on the move, continually seeking fresh grazing lands for his beasts. Nomad herdsmen used their animals to help them carry their goods.

The idea probably sprang up in many parts of the world about the same time. People in different countries used different animals, including horses, mules, asses, yaks, camels, reindeer, sheep, goats, oxen, buffaloes, and elephants. The modern horse, the best of all transport animals, did not reach America until the Spaniards brought it 400 years ago. The native horses and camels of North America had all died out thousands of years before. When Europeans arrived on the American continent, they found dog teams working with the northern Eskimos; and in the Peruvian Andes, the strange, long-necked, delicate-footed llama was used to draw loads.

Pack animals of all kinds are still used today. A dog can pull a 100-pound load, and a llama can carry the same weight on its back. A yak can carry 240 pounds, a pony 200 pounds, and a camel sometimes twice as much. Sheep and goats can carry 40 pounds, while an elephant can lift a ton. For many thousands of years, animals remained man's chief source of power on land. Unlike the steam engine☞, tractor☞, or automobile☞, they provided valuable extras—meat, milk, clothing,

A simple Indian travois: *two trailing tent poles supporting a platform.*

furs, and dried dung for their owners' fires. They needed no expensive fuels to run on, but could browse on the wayside grass. They could also breed and multiply their numbers.

Before man began to live with his fellows in small communities, he had no roadways other than animal tracks. The animal was man's first pathfinder. In dense jungle or desert, where a man could easily become lost, the animal's keen sense of smell often led the way to the nearest water hole.

In Africa, the elephant swept broad trails through the jungle. The rhinoceros trampled a matted reed path on its journey to the mud holes where it bathed. On the open veld, where the grass grew high, antelopes and zebras trekked from water hole to water hole, stamping out a track with their hooves. Countless generations followed the same trail.

Such tracks were far older than man. When he arrived, he followed these animal roadways. They led him to water and also to food, for water holes made good hunting grounds. They often showed him, too, the best way across mountains, or the best place to ford a river. American Indians learned to follow the bison, whose wide, well-beaten migration trails led the way across North America's Appalachian Mountains, always following the gentlest slopes.

Animal tracks were often the quickest way, but they seldom ran very straight. If a tree crashed across a jungle path, animals and men would make a new path around it. Years would pass. The tree trunk would rot and vanish. But the bend in many such tracks would remain, and the

roundabout route became permanent. As centuries passed, hunters still followed the same ancient paths. Such zigzagging tracks still criss-cross Africa today, beaten into smooth ruts in the jungle floor, making turns and twists for no apparent reason, avoiding obstacles that have long since vanished.

River banks and dry river beds, as well as animal tracks, provided man with roads. Many sleek modern roads and railroads are laid on top of these primitive trails. The Cumberland Gap, first reconnoitered by the bison, is now an American railroad gateway to the West.

These valley trails are by far nature's most ancient routes. Indeed, there were river valleys on this earth long before there were living creatures. After the animals came man, hunting and fishing; then the trader, driving his laden beasts. Settlements grew up by the river crossings on packhorse trails. From these, townships grew and prospered. At last came the modern highways and railroads, linking the towns with one another. It is interesting to remember, as we pass by in our automobiles, that we may be following the trail of some ancient hunter.

The coming of trade laid the foundations of man's first permanent roads. While man was wandering in search of food or plunder, or driving his cattle to graze, he was likely to follow haphazard routes. But later, as he took to farming and industry, he began to settle in towns and villages. He might then become quite rich in certain goods, yet lack others. He might grow too much corn, yet need certain materials for new tools; elsewhere, people with an excess of these materials may have been hungry. So instead of risking their lives robbing each other, such groups hit on the sensible idea of trading goods they had in plenty for others that they needed. So trade and permanent tradeways were born.

Perhaps the earliest and best-defined tradeway was the 700-mile-long amber route that crossed prehistoric Europe from the Mediterranean to the Baltic Sea. Amber is the fossilized gum of certain pine trees, many of which once grew in the great Baltic forests. It is golden, translucent, and looks rather like glass. People of early civilizations valued amber highly, for they thought it had magic powers.

Elsewhere in the world, other early civilizations were trading many lightweight goods overland. The Persians prized the gem known as lapis lazuli, both as an ornament and for its blue pigment, which the women used as an eye shadow. Lapis lazuli is rare, and the Persians must have brought it along a trade route, some 5000 years ago.

At a very early date, the Chinese learned to spin silk from the cocoons of a moth. For centuries they kept the process secret, but traded their silk with Persia by a Central Asian route, 3000 miles long.

In the Stone Age, cattle were traded overland. Southern England's ridgeways were originally cattle trails that ran above the swampy forests of the lowlands, and many can still be seen today. We can date

Top, how some ancient animal trails became modern highways. Right, early trade routes between the Mediterranean and amber lands. Far right, a piece of amber.

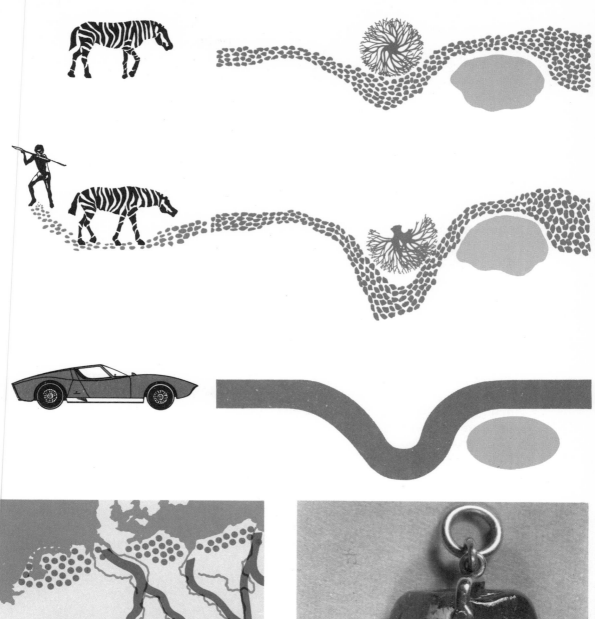
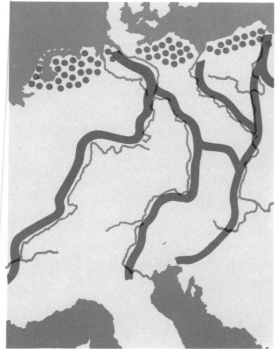

such trails by measuring the depth of the grooves they have worn. Some tracks in limestone are as much as 10 feet deep, which means that they may be over 6000 years old.

Early trade routes sound impressive, but they were little more than tracks. Though men crossed marshy ground, probably on log roads, they had not advanced far in the art of bridge-building. When they could not ford a river, they crossed it on rafts. In spite of these difficulties, archaeological remains prove that trade took place.

The next step in transport came when man invented vehicles to move heavy loads. Human porters and pack animals could carry only a limited amount. Early man must have learned that it was easier to drag certain things than to carry them. The first land vehicle, the sled, was one of man's earliest devices that overcame gravity and friction.

Gravity pulls you downward, and friction acts as a brake. The combination of these two forces makes it hard to move a burden. It is gravity that holds you to the earth when you walk, while friction keeps you from sliding about, because tiny bits of roughness on your shoes catch in minute points and hollows in the ground. A smooth slide eases the task of moving loads.

Although early man did not have our understanding of gravity and friction, he certainly knew their effects. People found that a deer killed during the hunt was easier to move when they dragged it than when they carried it—and that it dragged more easily on smooth ground.

There were two ways in which they could lessen the effect of friction. They might make the ground smoother; or they might smooth the bottom surface of the thing they dragged. The second method was obviously the easier.

At first, perhaps, Stone-Age people pulled a slaughtered animal to camp by dragging it along the ground; or, if there were two men, they probably carried the animal supported on a pole. But when one man faced the task of bringing two or more large animals back to camp, he must have dragged them on smooth hides. Eventually he would find that the smoother the "vehicle," the easier it was to move. People experimented, and made runners of bone or horn for a simple wooden sled.

Men living in forest areas soon learned to make artificial "horn" runners from smooth branches. At least 7000 years ago, they shaped the world's first sleds; some still survive, preserved in deep peat bogs. Early sled-builders also made runners for their own feet—the smooth soles of the wooden ski, one of the earliest records of which is a stone carving of a skier made about 4000 years ago.

Sleds still provide man with the easiest way of moving loads in lands where snow or swamp offer smooth surfaces that are too soft for the wheel. Eskimos squirt mouthfuls of water on their sled runners. In the arctic air, the water freezes, giving a superb, smooth running-surface.

An Eskimo sled; its polished runners glide easily over the surface of the ice.

16

A kind of sled was also used in Egypt more than 4000 years ago to move blocks of stone and great statues weighing many tons. Teams of workers hauled these colossal weights. A man with a pitcher poured water on the runners of the sled. It helped to smooth the rough ground that caused the friction—in short, it served as a lubricant. We use oil for the same purpose these days.

Now came perhaps man's greatest invention—the wheel. This occurred at least 5500 years ago, and it changed our world completely. Without it we should still be dragging loads on sleds.

The wheel seems simple, as do many great inventions. But imagine a world without it. How would you set about inventing one? You would have nothing around you to give you the idea, because the rolling wheel does not exist in nature.

Who first thought of it? We do not know. Its shape might have been suggested by the sun and the moon as they moved across the sky. In early days the sun was sacred; and so, at first, was the wheel.

Why does the wheel make moving easy? It almost entirely solves the problem of friction. A moving sled is held back by friction along the length of both its sliding runners. The wheel does not slide; its surface rolls bit by bit along the ground, so there is relatively little friction at each point of contact.

Perhaps people took the first step from sled to wheeled cart when they used log rollers. The Egyptians and the ancient Britons used a system of logs to move heavy blocks of stone. It took less effort to roll logs than to

How wheels may have developed from log rollers. Rollers may have been hollowed for easier movement, and later divided into two rollers on an axle.

pull a sled, but rollers presented problems of their own. While a roller four feet round moves one foot forward, a stone block resting on it travels only two feet forward; and fresh rollers must be placed beneath the stone block all the time to stop the block toppling over. The problem was how to anchor the rollers to the load. Perhaps its solution led to the world's first cart.

Archaeologists found the world's oldest known wheels in the land of Sumer. The most ancient Sumerian wheels we know consist of three flat wooden pieces pegged together to make a solid disk. Sumerian craftsmen fixed such wheels to axles. If they moved freely on their axles, the wheel hubs must have set up friction. (Today, we reduce friction by fitting ball bearings between hub and axle.) Friction also quickly wore out the wooden rims of the earliest wheels, but Sumerian craftsmen soon learned to protect the rims with copper nails.

In time, Sumer's wheels rolled around the ancient world. Eventually, craftsmen improved the wooden wheel by adding a metal tire and replacing the solid disk with light, strong spokes. Although the design of the wheel has changed little over the past 3000 years, its uses have multiplied many, many times.

How did people first put wheels to work? Simply by adding them to existing sleds and travois, just as the first automobile was an engine added to a carriage. Wheeled vehicles in the beginning were expensive and rare. People used them almost entirely for religious purposes, or for making war. We find the remains of early funeral carts in royal tombs. Perhaps the wheel was a mark of royal rank.

	3000 B.C.	2000 B.C.		A.D. 1	A.D. 1000	
Mesopotamia	○ ○	⊕ ⊕	⊕	⊕	⊕	
Asia	◉ ◉	◉	◉	◉	◉	◉
Mediterranean		◉ ⊕	⊕	⊕	⊕	
Europe			⊕ ⊕	⊕	⊕	
America					⊕	

The map shows the home of the wheel and how it spread across Europe.

Chart: when wheels were first used in different parts of the world.

As people made more wheeled vehicles, they began to use them to carry everyday loads: farm produce from fields to city markets, and manure and fodder about the farm. Thus wheels eased the work of man and beast, and encouraged the spread of commerce. But the first carts were crude and heavy, and they did not travel far. The clumsy oxen, yoked two abreast on either side of a single pole, moved slowly; and there were no good roads or wide bridges☞.

Better vehicles were introduced by the Romans. Their vast new empire, ranging from Britain to Africa, depended on travel and transport. The Roman *caretta*, a two-wheeled vehicle, gives us our own word "cart." *Vehiculum* meant simply "something that carries."

To make a fast journey alone, you used the light *birota*—the sports car of those days. If you traveled with your family, you might use the *carruca*, a kind of covered wagon, which carried a much heavier load.

Despite improvements in the ways they built their chariots and carts, people were slow to make proper harness for their horses. Horses remained half-choked by the breast bands, girth bands, yoke, and pole designed for oxen 3000 years before. But some pictures show Roman horses harnessed between shafts and wearing padded collars. This more efficient use of horse power advanced both the speed and the range of transport.

For all their many skills, the Romans did not know how to build a four-wheeled cart with a swiveling front axle to help turn sharp corners. Perhaps Rome's barbaric Celtic foes were the first to make such an articulated wagon.

As wheeled vehicles became more numerous, men were forced to build better roads. But good roads cannot be built by one family or tribe: vast organizations are needed. Good roads meant more trade for merchants, and easier control of empires for rulers.

In Peru, on the west coast of South America, the Inca rulers created amazing mountain roads. One stretched for more than 2000 miles from north to south of the Inca kingdom.

Ancient China also developed a fine road system. Several hundred years before the birth of Christ, the Chou emperors kept a highways commissioner. The Chinese had five grades of roads, from the narrow *ching*, a pathway wide enough for man and beast, to the broad *lu*, which could take three wagons abreast.

Along China's great roads, many of which were paved, merchants carried silk to Persia. There, another highway helped to speed the woven material to Rome, where it might bring as much as $200, or £75, a pound. King Cyrus, who lived 2500 years ago, had created Persia's great empire. He policed a fine system of trackways, where stage-posts at regular intervals housed supplies of fresh horses. Cyrus's messengers could speed on horse or by camel at almost 100 miles a day.

The greatest of all the early roads were undoubtedly those of Rome. At one time, Roman roads stretched in a 53,000-mile network from Ethiopia to the north of England. Armies and trade flowed along this huge system to protect and enrich the Empire. The roads were paved, like those the Romans found in Carthage, and they also had horse relay stations, like those of Persia. No better roads than Rome's were built until a century ago.

There are some kinds of country where it is difficult to build roads, and a dry, sandy desert is one of them. Sand is shifting, and it blows like snow; roads require firm foundations.

For this reason, wheels did not penetrate into Africa's great northern deserts until recent times. Yet these hot, sandy wastes proved no barrier to transport. Merchants have been using desert tradeways for centuries. Caravans of pack animals—first the ox, then the camel—trudging in single file, regularly set out across the blistering Sahara to link the wealth of Central Africa with Europe.

Inland, along the northern edge of the desert, lay a string of cities like seaports. There was a similar line in the south. Between them the sand lay in waves like the sea. The camel was the ship that crossed it.

The camel is well adapted to desert life. Its splayed feet do not sink deeply into the sand, as would a horse's hooves, and it has an extraordinary ability to conserve water. In addition, its hump is full of spare supplies of fat, which enable it to travel many miles without food. A camel can carry 300 pounds at a steady four miles an hour. Camels can supply their drivers with milk, meat, hair for making tents, and dried dung for burning on cold desert nights. In these ways, the camel made it possible for men to trade across a desert.

The height of this desert traffic saw camel trains of as many as 10,000 to 15,000 beasts. Their cargoes to the Mediterranean included gold, ivory, copper, gum, civet, scent, and slaves. They brought back cloth, beads, brassware, spices, and sugar.

The keepers of the early camel routes were the Tuareg tribesmen, to whom this desert was home. They dug and maintained the important water wells, and provided guides along the way. A guide was always necessary in these featureless wastes and, strangely enough, many of them were blind. They kept to the trails by smelling the sand—which is the way animals follow each other. For many centuries the Tuaregs controlled the desert routes, charging tolls to the merchants who used them. They kept the Sahara open, protected the travelers, and kept Africa in touch with Europe.

One thousand years ago a holy war brought Arab Moslems into West Africa. Arab merchants wrested trade from the Tuaregs. For

Above, principal Roman roads in A.D. 200, from Western Europe to the Far East. Below, camel train; some still use desert tradeways trodden in ancient times.

almost 500 years these merchants made the North African desert routes some of the richest and most important in the world. From Constantine to Kano, and from Tlemcen to Timbuktu, Arab camels ferried enormous wealth. The desert villages grew into cities. At the height of its prosperity, Timbuktu boasted 100,000 inhabitants. People journeyed many hundred miles to see the city that blossomed in the desert.

Soon after 1400, Portuguese seamen, exploring Africa's west coast, found a new way to transport its wealth. A single ship could carry as much as 1500 camels—and it could travel faster. The sea route bypassed the Sahara. People began to make less use of overland trails. So ships of the desert gave place to ships of the sea.

The deserts of Northwest Africa prevented travel from improving in that region. In Europe, man-made wars and ways of life slowed down travel throughout the Middle Ages. For more than a thousand years after the decay of the Roman Empire, there was little advance in land transport or road making. Monks and pilgrims moved overland on horseback, but few people traveled far with heavy loads. A Roman official of A.D. 100 could travel faster overland than Queen Elizabeth in the late 16th century.

In summer the trackways might remain quite firm, but in winter they turned into bogs. People despoiled or neglected the paved Roman roads. Villagers prized up their stones for building. A story tells how someone dug clay from the middle of a road to make bricks. That night a passing traveler fell into the hole and broke his neck.

On these wet, broken roads, heavy cart wheels caused chaos, churning the mud like porridge. As trade increased, the country ways grew worse, for they were forced to bear more traffic. Ten-horse teams struggled desperately in the mire to haul their lumbering four-ton wagons. Wealthy noblemen suffered like any peasant when their ornate carriages overturned in the mud. Great droves of cattle, often numbering several thousand, did not improve the surfaces either. But as the roads were free to all, and often used by strangers, no one person, or parish, or local government, felt obliged to pay for their upkeep.

By 1600 things had begun to improve. Trade throughout Europe flourished. Villages grew into towns, and towns into cities. People had more money, and demanded better transport. In 1662, a service of horse-drawn buses☞ was introduced into the streets of Paris. The *Carrosses à Cinq Sous* seated eight, ran to a timetable, charged a flat rate of five sous however far you went, and made the journey whether they were full or empty. This was the first public omnibus system in history.

In 1663 Britain passed the first Turnpike Act, by which all road users were required to pay a fee or toll to be used for improving the roads. Better roads encouraged faster travel. Stagecoaches, fixed on springs instead of swung from leather straps, carried passengers and mail,

Upper, an early steam locomotive built in 1853. Center, a modern Canadian train propelled by gas turbines. Lower, a modern monorail train.

rattling across the country-side at speeds of up to eight miles an hour. Drivers changed horses at posting inns, like the Romans 1500 years before them. By 1830, one British coach owner could boast 3000 coaches and 150,000 horses.

In the early 19th century, stagecoaches helped to open up the North American continent. Wells Fargo and Overland Mail coaches, following the mule trains and covered wagons of the settlers, regularly crossed 2500 miles of forest, plain, and mountain, carrying people, parcels, mail—and even oysters. The light, fast riders of the Pony Express, changing their mounts at frequent intervals, kept up speeds of over 10 miles an hour. Despite Indians, outlaws, floods, and prairie fires, wheels and horse power—and the old Persian stage system—were opening a new world to the people of Europe.

Increasing travel opened people's eyes to vast new lands. Yet as recently as a century and a half ago, land transport still moved no faster than it had done under the Romans. Man relied chiefly on the muscle power of beasts; the only other source of power he possessed was the natural thrust of wind and water.

Windmills pumped water, and sometimes ground corn. Watermills ground corn and worked factories. But wind and water were unreliable; a drought or a calm day could bring work to a standstill.

As trade and industry increased, man built artificial waterfalls to drive his wheels, and began to invent strange machines to pump water to higher levels. From these early devices emerged the idea that was at last to revolutionize transport.

The idea was steam—a product of water charged with the energy of heat. About 1650, men began experimenting with steam in attempts to pump up water. An early inventor, Thomas Savery, made several machines. In one, he forced steam into a closed container, then cooled it, turning the steam back into water. This water took up less space than the original steam. The container had become part vacuum. Savery's vacuum could suck up water from a mining shaft to the surface.

Thomas Newcomen (1663–1729) made a different kind of engine. Steam helped to push a piston up inside a cylinder. Rods connected to the piston helped to pump up water. Then James Watt (1736–1819) made an engine in which steam pushed a piston both up and down. Movable rods linked Watt's pistons to wheels and turned them around. Watt's engines powered sawmills.

If steam could turn wheels in sawmills, why should it not turn the wheels of vehicles? In 1769, the Frenchman Cugnot, using steam, produced the first self-propelled carriage. In 1804, Richard Trevithick of Cornwall built the first really powerful steam locomotive☞. It pulled a 10-ton load (at a walking pace) along a 10-mile cast-iron tramway in Wales. From these beginnings stemmed modern railroads.

One of the world's first automobiles, Karl Benz's "horseless carriage" of 1888.

24

Railroads, as such, were not new in history. The ancient Greeks moved heavy loads along ruts worn in rock. In 16th-century European mines, men drew trucks along wooden rails. But the modern railroad was born in the deep, rich collieries of northern England, when the steam locomotive gave new meaning to the rail trackway. And from the mines themselves came the power the locomotive needed—the coal to build up a head of steam.

Since the beginning of history, no man had traveled any faster than the horse. The steam locomotive provided the breakthrough. At first it traveled slower than a horse, but it could pull far heavier loads. In 1829, Stephenson's *Rocket* moved at 15 miles an hour. By 1850, locomotives moved five times faster.

Locomotives began by drawing freight. Soon, they were pulling passenger coaches. In 1830, the world's first passenger railroad opened on Britain's Liverpool and Manchester Line. The passengers sat in a series of compartments that were like stagecoaches joined together. The noise and speed were frightening at first, but were very soon accepted.

Railroads proved to be fast and cheap, and people flocked to use them. By 1843, Britain had laid 2000 miles of track. In two years the mileage doubled. The railroad began to transform the country, throwing bridges and viaducts across pastoral valleys, and driving cuttings through sleepy fields. It gave birth to new cities. It moved whole populations about.

Top, a Rolls Royce of 1913. Lower, a radar-controlled automobile of the future.

Beginning in Britain, railroads soon spread throughout the world. In 1869, in the heart of America, Chinese tracklayers from the West Coast met Irish laborers from the East Coast. The Union Pacific Railroad had spanned the continent. Today, unbroken railroads stretch still farther. You can buy a ticket in Paris that will take you to Pyongyang, North Korea—a journey of about 9000 miles.

The railroad changed man's life, and drew his world closer; it even altered his eating habits. Fish from the coasts and fresh food from the farms could be speeded to cities. People could open new lands that had previously lain idle, such as the corn belts and the stockraising prairies. Refrigerated rail trucks☞ carried thousands of tons of freshly killed meat to market. Industrial populations could safely double in size, but still be fed and distribute their goods.

Today, locomotives are moving more goods than ever. At the iron mines of Minnesota, for instance, 13,000-ton freight trains—equal to 135,000 camel loads—are not an uncommon sight. But cheaper, cleaner, more efficient oil-burning diesels☞ and electric-driven locomotives have largely replaced steam and coal. Electric trains can accelerate far more rapidly, and they do not have to carry their fuel. Electric cable cars can climb a one-in-two gradient. Electric motors drive our subways and undergrounds.

Fast modern cars hurtle round the track at Daytona, U.S.A.

What was happening to road travel while the railroad spread across the world? Road transport developed slowly at first. Steam power was far better suited to large vehicles that traveled on rails.

The first practical steam carriage, invented 40 years before Trevithick's rail locomotive, was designed by Cugnot as a road vehicle. But its boiler was too small to raise much steam. It had to stop repeatedly for water.

Steam did not solve road travel problems. Many 19th-century steam coaches were slow and heavy. Their unwieldy engines took up much space. Furthermore, they frightened people and broke up the roads. Turnpike owners charged them high tolls. By 1840 few remained.

But people continued to experiment with horseless carriages. They tried to fit an engine's fire-box, boiler, and cylinder within a smaller space, enclosed by lighter metal. They tried to make a smaller, yet stronger, engine. They tried new forms of power—gas and electricity.

In 1859, Étienne Lenoir made an engine in which gas replaced steam. An electric spark jumped across a cylinder and ignited a gas within it. The exploding gas of this *internal-combustion*☞ engine pushed a piston. But this method proved as expensive as steam; people still sought a cheaper, more efficient fuel to give greater punch to the piston.

What they found at last was petroleum, trapped in natural reservoirs underground. In 1882, Gottlieb Daimler used vaporized petroleum to drive a piston much faster than Lenoir's. In 1885, Daimler fixed such an engine to a wooden bicycle, and so invented the motorcycle☞. In the same year Karl Benz powered a tricycle with a single-cylinder engine; it could travel at 8 miles an hour. In 1894, an automobile won a race by speeding at 15 miles an hour.

New inventions followed one another fast. Plentiful petroleum and good cheap steel, together with the mass-production methods of Henry Ford, meant a sudden flooding of the roads with automobiles. Rubber, and new ways of treating it, led to pneumatic tires and smoother riding.

People first thought of automobiles as "horseless carriages," and built them in just that shape. Streamlining began as speeds increased, and wheels got smaller. Wars developed new kinds of automobiles, such as tracklayers, gun carriages, and troop carriers. From these sprang farm tractors☞, trucks, and buses. Automobiles evolved like animals, but in decades rather than in millions of years.

At first, the automobile was a luxury. In 1899, in the United States, 600 had been built and sold. By 1925, the number approached 20 million. Today you can choose from a huge range of models, some costing 25 times the price of others—some able to do 12 miles, others 50, to the gallon. In 1967 alone, General Motors of America sold nearly 5 million vehicles. It is said that there are enough automobiles in Britain and America to carry their combined populations.

Flyover crossings on the San Bernardino Freeway at El Monte, California.

We have seen how rail transport changed the outlook of the world. Road transport has changed it again. Motels, fuel stations, factories, oil refineries, and even the roads themselves, all spring from the automobile. Long-distance trailer trucks are stealing much freight from the railroads. Highway coaches, with speeds of up to 80 miles an hour, are also taking away many of the railroads' passengers.

The automobile would have found it hard going on the old mud roads or rutted cart tracks. A Scot, Macadam, 150 years ago pioneered one of the first smooth road surfaces. He laid down a mixture of stone chips and asphalt, which was also designed to keep out water. Tarmac and concrete are the chief road surfaces today, providing tire-grip and smoothness on speedways.

The limit of stagecoach travel used to be about 100 miles a day. Now a man and his family can easily do 500 miles a day along the German *autobahns* or the United States turnpikes.

First-class modern highways are built to suit the needs of the automobile; they are angled and banked so that the vehicle half steers itself. Future roads may control the automobile altogether. Russia has a plan for an electronic highway that would both propel and steer the vehicle. You would preselect your speed and the distance you wished to travel, then sleep, if you wished, until you got there.

Has the automobile reached its limits? It depends almost entirely on roads and on parking space. In the vast open lands of Russia and America, fine new highways can develop freely. But in much of old Europe, more cars mean less speed. In ancient towns many well-surfaced roads must remain no wider than carriage ways designed for horse and cart. Small nations, such as Britain, can produce one and a half million automobiles a year, but cannot spare land for wider roads to carry them. For speedy travel in the future, men may have to look elsewhere—to water and to the air.

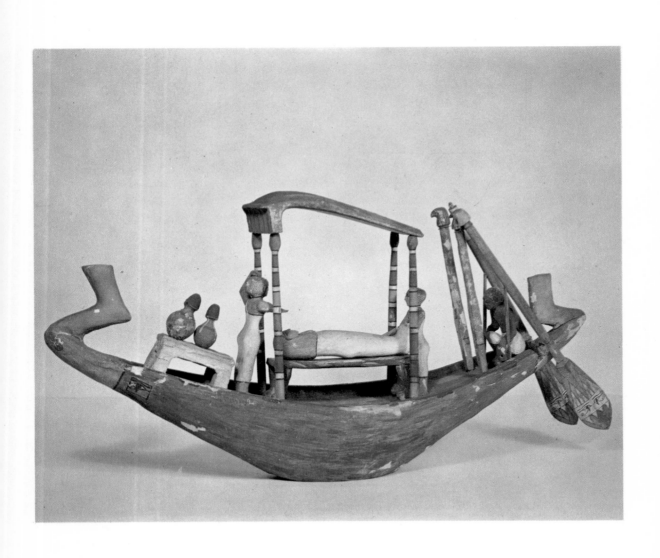

3 Man Spans the Oceans

Water covers two thirds of our planet. Without it, life in its splendid variety could not exist. The first living things were water creatures. All land animals, including man, evolved from them. But man cannot breathe the oxygen in water, nor can he swim as easily as mammals adapted to aquatic life. Man has always liked to live near water, because it refreshes him and gives him food. Yet early in man's history, water was a barrier that cut him off from much of the world.

Over the years, man has invented many ways of traveling on water. Yet long before human beings had evolved, water creatures were moving themselves about by many of the same methods. Man has simply "re-invented" the oarsmanship of the water beetle and the squid's jet propulsion☞.

Man learns by watching, imitating, and adapting. He must often have seen logs and reeds floating down his rivers—sometimes with animals on them. He must have seen drowned carcasses too.

His first vessel, no doubt, was just a floating log. He may have straddled it and guided it with his feet and hands. But a log is unstable, and it rolls over easily. In time, people found that several logs lashed together make a steady platform, or raft. In Egypt they built rafts out of bundles of reeds. Elsewhere, people hollowed out logs to make dugout canoes. The dugout was better balanced, because its center of gravity was lower, and it was more easily steered than a raft.

People living in the Middle East learned to use animal carcasses, blown up like water wings. They stretched animal skins over wicker frames to make the primitive craft we call *coracles*. In time, more elaborate boats appeared: log rafts buoyed up on inflated skins. The coracle, reed boat, and dugout canoe were man's earliest vessels.

Man first took to water on lakes, rivers, and estuaries. As early as the New Stone Age, people began moving over lakes and rivers for trade. In time, great civilizations grew up beside river highways.

Ancient Egyptian model of a barge carrying a dead pharaoh to his tomb.

The shapes of early vessels varied with the materials of which they were made. Forest people built dugout canoes—tree trunks hollowed out with axes and fire. On treeless plains, inflated animal skins were often the only means of floating across rivers. People combined animal hides and riverside plants to make light, shell-like coracles. Along Egypt's Nile, where the papyrus reeds grew, people made reed-bundle boats or *baris*. Bound reeds formed both floor and sides of the vessel, which was curved like an open banana skin. The high prows of Venetian gondolas owe their shape to these early reed boats, whose tightly bound bundles were drawn sharply out of the water at stem and stern. Often a taut rope or "hogging truss" ran the length of the boat and kept the ends from sagging.

In spite of the various materials and designs they used, early men did not know *why* boats floated. They knew that a stone would sink, while a piece of wood would float. But they did not understand the principle of density—that an object bulk for bulk heavier (and therefore denser) than water will sink, while one lighter than water will float.

Early men knew that wicker baskets and animal hides easily became waterlogged and sank. But trial and error showed that a wicker basket frame, covered with stretched hide, and daubed with waterproof pitch or bitumen, would float and even carry heavy weights. People noticed that a loaded coracle sat lower in the water than an empty one. But its upturned sides still prevented it sinking.

The first boat-builders were familiar with these effects, but were unaware of the principles underlying them. Today, with scientific knowledge of the laws of buoyancy, we can take great steel plates that, separately, would sink like a stone, and weld them on frames into giant "coracles"—ocean liners☞ weighing thousands of tons.

How did the first boatmen move their craft on the water? In the beginning, no doubt, the log boat or raft merely carried a man downstream. He floated along with the current, but he had to walk back. The first steering appliance was perhaps a single pole, a kind of extension of the arm. Then someone may have found that this pole, or oar, if moved rapidly from side to side, could also push the boat forward. People would have noticed the tails of fishes, and the webbed feet of frogs and water birds. By broadening the ends of their steering poles into paddles—the equivalent of webbed feet and fishes' tails—people learned to paddle against a current.

Perhaps on some gusty day a Stone-Age man discovered that the force of the wind would drive both him and his boat without paddling. People began experimenting, raising "sails" to catch the wind, which they found would drive their boats without any effort on their part. In time, with sail or oars, according to conditions, people could often take their boats wherever they liked.

Ancient Egyptian trading ship carrying resins, ivory, leopard skins, and apes.

With simple boats, many people have transformed a water barrier into a way of life. Today, boats like the world's earliest craft still carry people across rivers in remote parts of the world. In certain lands, people have produced versions of such boats to suit special needs.

One of the most remarkable of these boats is the Eskimo's *kayak*. With this slender, speedy little hunting craft he catches salmon, seal, walrus, and sometimes even whales.

The Eskimo spends much of his life on frozen soil where few plants grow. He must hunt and fish to survive. Nearly all his food, clothing, tools, and weapons come from the animals he kills. So does his kayak. In structure, it is a development of the coracle. The Eskimo builds its long pointed frame from light struts of driftwood or whalebone, which he binds together with sealskin thongs. Finally, he wraps a patchwork of sealskins, tightly sewn together, around the frame. The skins entirely cover the frame except for a small manhole into which the Eskimo squeezes, plugging the hole with his body.

Secure in his cockpit, the Eskimo becomes one with his craft. With a flick of his short, double-ended paddle he can dart rapidly about, tunnel through a wave, or even roll right over in the wave's path. The kayak is so light that the Eskimo can carry it over any land or ice barrier in his way.

Apart from the *kayak*, which means "man's boat," Eskimos have an *umiak* or "woman's boat," which is also derived from the coracle. These large, wood-framed, skin-sided, open vessels can carry a dozen people with their goods. Eskimos use them when moving camp. If they are cut off by ice, they may turn an umiak upside down and spend the winter under it.

Elsewhere in the world, simple boats turn rivers into tradeways. Ecuadorian peasants living in the upland rain forests make a huge raft

from balsa trees, build a light wooden shelter on it, and float downstream with their wives and families until they reach the estuary of the river Guayas. There they break up the raft and sell the logs to dealers. Then they travel back to their forests by rail to chop down more trees and start all over again.

In China, where there are several great river highways, many people have made simple waterborne homes. *Junks* and *sampans*, all jammed together, stretch up the rivers for miles, forming huge floating cities where people could live, raise families, and die without once setting foot on land.

In ancient times most ships simply followed the rivers or hugged the shallow coastline of seas. But about A.D. 400 occurred one of history's most amazing sea epics—the ocean migration of the Polynesians.

These mysterious people left their homes in Asia and sailed their canoes out into the vast Pacific. In time they covered southeast Asia's islands. Still they kept on going. Today their descendants, and their plants and animals—breadfruit, chickens, and hogs—thrive throughout the Pacific islands.

After some centuries the Polynesians reached Tahiti. From Tahiti, whole families fearlessly set their prows again toward the unknown. For 1600 miles they sailed across the cloudless, landless ocean, until a long white cloud on the horizon led them to the land that lay beneath it. The land was New Zealand, and the descendants of these people are the Maoris who live there today. They still call New Zealand *Aotea-roa*, which means "the long white cloud."

Why did the Polynesians undertake these tremendous voyages? No one really knows. Perhaps warlike invaders drove them out of Asia. Whatever the reason, without the help of metal tools, or a magnetic compass, they successfully sailed their open boats all over the Pacific Ocean.

What were these boats? They were simple dugout canoes, but often huge ones 70 feet long, with built-up wooden sides. Two centuries ago, Captain Cook saw some that held as many as 100 men each. We read of occasions when 800 people voyaged on a *catamaran*—a platform lashed across two canoes.

The Polynesians lashed their canoes together for a special reason. Many Pacific islands are coral atolls—a broken necklace of coral strung around a calm lagoon. To sail inside means crossing submerged reefs that could rip the bottom out of a boat. A deep keel, like a yacht's, designed to balance its tall sails, would be useless in coral waters. The Polynesians used sails, but dared not have deep keels to prevent their craft from capsizing. They did this by tying two canoes side by side. Later came single canoes supported by wooden floats—keels built outward instead of down. We call such vessels *outriggers*.

Upper, a pirate Viking ship of about A.D. 900, found at Gokstad in Norway. Lower, Spanish galleons in Lisbon harbor, as depicted by a 16th-century artist.

Both paddles and sails propelled these outriggers. But the trade winds and sea currents that circle the Pacific must have played a greater part. We know that ships from Japan have drifted as far as California, carried by wind and current alone. We remember how Thor Heyerdahl and his companions, on the balsa raft *Kon-Tiki*, drifted 4300 miles from Peru to the Polynesian island of Raroia. Heyerdahl believed that the Polynesians came from South America, not from Asia. Did he prove his theory? Perhaps not. But the Polynesians are there, and they have peopled the Pacific; how they did it is one of the great tales of man.

Without boats, man could move few goods over water. Boats increased man's power and extended his horizons. Boats and the cargoes they carried helped man to grow rich and to raise great cities.

About 3500 years ago, the world's first great sea trading expedition set out from the Egyptian Nile. At the command of Queen Hatshepsut, a fleet of large ships sailed to "Punt"—what may now be Somaliland. The sailors returned with a priceless cargo, of which we still have records. It included myrrh, fragrant woods, ivory, gold, eye cosmetics, apes, and slaves.

Queen Hatshepsut's wooden ships were far more seaworthy than the early reed river boats. But Egypt lacked trees for timber. She had to trade for wood with the Phoenicians in Syria, where cedars grew.

These cedar forests helped the Phoenicians to increase their power. By 1200 B.C. they were using cedar wood to build large fleets of their own. They had two coastal strongholds, the ports of Tyre and Sidon. They also had great courage and an eye for trade. Slowly the Phoenicians began probing into unknown seas, carrying trinkets and Tyrian dyes, seeking always in return that on which they based their power: copper, tin, iron, silver, and gold.

Very soon, the Phoenicians had trading colonies throughout the Mediterranean, in Cyprus, Crete, and Spain. Guided at night by the

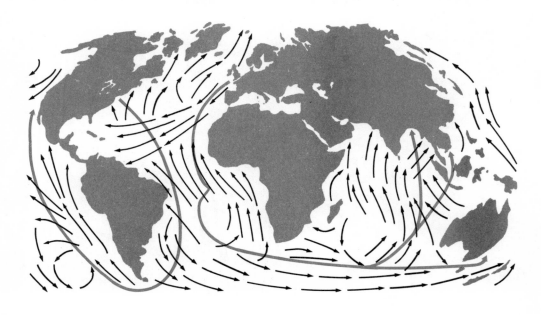

stars, hugging the coastlines by day, they pushed out into the wild Atlantic, made their way north to Britain, where they traded for tin, and perhaps even reached the Baltic. For over 500 years, these Phoenicians from Syria were the greatest merchant sailors in the world.

By 500 B.C. the Phoenician city of Carthage, in North Africa, had a population of half a million. Its merchant sailors continued to explore the unknown, still seeking new colonies and trade. One ancient record tells how they sailed around Africa—2000 years before Vasco da Gama. Another tells how an expedition of 60 ships, with 30,000 people, sailed from Carthage to start new colonies down the then little-known coast of West Africa.

At last, the rising city of Rome threatened the might of Carthage. The Carthaginians replied by ferrying elephants into Spain. Hannibal marched them over the Alps into Italy, where he and his elephants defeated the Romans. But it was the last victory for Carthage. That great city, with its half a million people, was soon destroyed by Rome.

The days of the Phoenician sea traders were over; they were beaten in part by one of their own inventions, for Roman carpenters had built copies of a great Carthaginian warship that had been washed up on a Roman shore. This may have been a *pentere* or a *quinquereme*, a ram-headed galley rowed by 300 oarsmen arranged in banks of 5.

Apart from Roman descriptions of the quinquereme, few clues remain to help us picture the ships of Carthage. The Carthaginians were a secretive people; they kept their trade routes hidden, and would rather scuttle their ships than allow them to fall into the hands of their rivals. But we do know that a plentiful supply of slaves provided the muscle power to drive their warships. We know that their merchant ships☞, with sails of papyrus or flax, could carry several hundred tons of goods. We know that these sails were little better than those used by the river boats of Egypt, which worked really well only in a following wind.

The Phoenicians were born seamen, and with their defeat sea transport dwindled. No better ships appeared for another 1000 years. Then came the small swift Arab *dhows*. Their lateen sails helped them move both with and against the wind. Unlike the sails of Carthage, these new sails ran the length of the hull☞, not across it. Arab seamen could so angle their lateen sail that the ship was driven forward by winds coming from either side, as well as from astern.

In A.D. 787, near Dorchester, in southern England, three strange ships appeared offshore. Unsuspectingly, the local sheriff walked down the beach to meet them. Fierce warriors leapt ashore and killed him and stayed to plunder nearby settlements. Then they set their dragon prows for home, hundreds of leagues across the stormy North Sea.

These people were Vikings, the great sea warriors who enriched themselves mainly by plunder. The raid of 787 gave their victims a taste

The map shows clipper routes (red); arrows represent winds prevailing in July.

Two Scottish-built clippers, the Taeping *and the* Ariel, *racing up the English Channel at the end of their 99-day voyage from China in the Tea Race of 1866*

of many raids to come—in Britain, France, Spain, and even Africa. The Vikings learned their seamanship in deep drowned river valleys— the fjords of Norway. Huge forests covered these valley slopes. Like the Phoenicians, the Vikings possessed little wealth besides timber. It made them some of the greatest seamen in history.

Thanks to the Viking custom of burying dead chieftains in their ships, some of these vessels have survived, preserved by clay and peat. King Olaf Geirstad-Alv's ship was buried with him more than 1100 years ago; it was over 70 feet long, displaced 20 tons of water, and was rowed by 32 oarsmen.

Unlike the spoon-shaped vessels of Egypt, Viking ships were built around a strong wooden frame. Ribs curved upward from the long stout keel in rather the same way as our ribs grow out from our backbone. Planks, clinched by nails, provided the watertight skin that was stretched around the ribs. The planks themselves overlapped like tiles. Tall, hardy, fair-haired Vikings manned the oars of these ships, set the great square sails, and worked the huge stern oars as rudders.

No one living on the coasts of northwest Europe was safe from Viking raids. Their silent warships, more fearful than tramping armies, gave no warning of their approach, and left no trail to be followed. In

Silhouettes representing six different types of sailing ship. Each type has its own distinctive combination of lateen and square-rigged sails.

their shallow vessels, the Vikings even rowed up rivers to attack Orléans, Paris, and London. Swedish Vikings sailed up Baltic rivers and down those of the Black Sea to attack Constantinople.

Viking ships set up new kingdoms as well as destroying old ones. The state that was to become Russia grew up around the Viking town of Novgorod. From a Norse settlement in France, Normans conquered England in A.D. 1,066. Vikings settled in far-off Iceland, and even in Greenland.

In A.D. 1001, Leif Ericsson sailed still farther west. He found a "Stoneland"; we call it Labrador. He found a "Woodland"; we call it Newfoundland. He found a "Vinland," which might be Massachusetts Bay. There, a Viking colony throve for several hundred years before native Indians drove it out. Five centuries went by before Columbus, sailing in a very different kind of ship, rediscovered the New World. Viking warriors had found the New World and lost it. Europe's explorer-traders rediscovered it, sailing in stouter ships with better navigational aids.

In the meantime, the power of the sea traders grew. In 1400, the island city of Venice was the known world's greatest port. Venetian merchant ships, meeting the land caravans from the East, loaded cargoes of spices, silks, and jewels, and sailed to Europe. Then Moslem Turks gained control of the Oriental land routes, making trade difficult for Christian merchants. They sought new sea routes to the eastern spice lands.

Spice was the lure that was to open up the world; the ships were to come from Portugal. Greatly improved ships and sailing methods owed much to Portugal's Prince Henry the Navigator, a scholar and scientist. He gathered learned Christians, Jews, and Arabs together to make new and better maps. Instruments derived from Arabian astrolabes measured the sun's height and gave seamen their north-south position. Improved compasses showed direction. The Portuguese developed a new kind of ship, the *caravel*, to coast down West Africa. It had two lateen sails, but the captains soon found that wind pressure on the foresails put a strain on the rudder. They eased the strain by adding a mizzenmast in the stern. Ships with two square sails and a lateen-rigged mizzen were known as *carracks*. Carracks and caravels opened the age of discovery.

In 1487, Bartholomeu Diaz rounded the southern tip of Africa. In 1492, Columbus unknowingly discovered the Bahamas. By 1499, Vasco da Gama had sailed to India and back again by way of Africa.

Soon Portuguese, Spanish, Dutch, and English were all finding new ways through the seas. Not all explorers had the best or the biggest of ships. In 1519, Magellan set off to sail around the globe. His five ships were "very old and patched" with ribs "as soft as butter." Only the *Vittoria*, a small ship of 90 tons, returned; but it was the first to circle the earth.

Long-distance trade followed the explorers. Merchants cried out for ever bigger ships to carry bigger and richer cargoes. Rival nations built warships like floating castles, armed with cannon to defend their traders. A single log had made a dugout canoe; now 2000 trees went to build one warship. Shipwrights also needed nails, spikes, chains, bolts, cables, ropes, marlines, pitch, tar, rosin, paint, spars, and anchors. Ship-building was no longer a task for one man, but an industry of many craftsmen.

After the great age of discovery, Europe's trading nations built up trading empires overseas. At first, Spanish galleons dominated the oceans. But after the defeat of the Armada, Britain's men-of-war and merchantmen grew numerous and powerful. The British East India Company gained control of India, a source of unbelievable wealth. Massive East India ships plied slowly between the Orient and Europe. Speed was no object. Their sails were furled at night. Britain's strong navy protected her merchants from the threat of faster competitors.

Then, in the 1830s, a new rival appeared in the form of the fast trading clipper. United States shipyards in Boston and Baltimore had

The Great Eastern, *launched in 1858. Her massive iron hull weighed 8000 tons.*

begun experimenting with frigates and packet boats that would outsail any craft then known. In 1832, Isaac McKim from Baltimore built a ship called the *Ann McKim*. Shaped like a small, fast schooner, it was twice a schooner's size; and at once it began to trade in the East. It started a trade war, a sea-racing rivalry between ships whose long, lean hulls ended in sharp bows that clipped the waves. Clipper ships carried clouds of canvas that caught the slightest breeze.

Clipper captains never furled their sails at night. They could not afford to. Their job was to outspeed their rivals: to be first in London with the tea crop from China, first in San Francisco with food for the gold miners, or first to Australia with gold prospectors. In 1850, people paid high prices for cargoes carried by the fastest ships. In a single trip a clipper could repay its construction costs.

The racing clipper in its heyday became one of the most beautiful and most complicated vehicles ever devised by man. Its many thousand square feet of sail needed many men to handle them. The 2421-ton *Sovereign of the Seas*, which sailed in 1852, required a crew of 105: 4 mates, 2 boatswains, 2 carpenters, 2 sailmakers, 3 stewards, 2 cooks, 80 seamen, and 10 boys.

These crews, often made up of adventurers and lawless rogues, made possible some of the fastest sailing speeds ever known. Clipper ships halved the voyage time from London to Australia. In 1854, the *Lightning* made a record run of 436 miles in 24 hours on a transatlantic crossing. Rival clipper ships, superbly built and navigated, would race each other over many thousands of miles. In 1852, the *John Gilpin* and the *Flying Fish* raced the 15,000 miles from New York to San Francisco at average speeds that differed by less than six seconds a mile.

These speeds owed much to seamanship and design. They also owed much to the sextant and the chronometer. These instruments, made

practicable in the 18th century, enabled seamen to determine latitude and longitude accurately. Clipper captains could also increase their speeds by studying charts of ocean currents and winds, prepared by Matthew Maury of the United States Navy.

In time, people devised new kinds of clippers. In 1853, Donald McKay built the 4555-ton *Great Republic*; the biggest merchantman of its day, it was more than twice the length of the pioneer clipper, *Ann McKim*. American clippers were wooden ships; the British built theirs of teak, oak, or elm, sheathed with copper to prevent damage from sea worm. In the 1840s, the British began building iron ships; later, steel masts and steel wire ropes, stronger and lighter than wood and hemp, were introduced.

The broad-sailed clippers were at the height of their glory after the first steamboats appeared. For some years the clippers out-raced the steamers. But the days of sail were numbered.

Just as rivers and seas are natural barriers to landsmen, land can be a barrier to watermen. In many countries men have overcome land barriers by cutting canals across them. Canals may be man-made rivers, or short cuts joining one body of water to another.

The idea of cutting artificial waterways is very old. In 1875 B.C., the Egyptian pharaoh Sesostris cut a short canal on the Nile to bypass some rapids that endangered his ships. About the same time, another pharaoh had a 100-mile canal dug to link the Nile with the Red Sea. It was originally made as a ditch for irrigation only. But Phoenician ships may have sailed along it about 600 B.C., when pharaoh Necho II sent them on a voyage around Africa. We read that in the days of the Persian king Darius the canal was 200 feet wide and 40 feet deep, and that once a fleet of 24 ships sailed along it.

Over the years this great canal was neglected. In time, it silted up and disappeared. But another, built about 1000 years ago in China, is maintained and used to this day. The Chinese and the Egyptians were pioneers in canal-building and much of their trade depended on transport along waterways.

The engineers who made artificial waterways found themselves faced with a big problem. How could they make water climb hills? People solved this problem when they invented locks. The Dutch and Italians, who often suffered from floods, learned to close stretches of river with timber lock gates. Then, in 1481, the Italian Domenico brothers turned these to an ingenious use. They built two lock gates some distance apart, separating two different levels of water in a river. The first gate was opened, and a ship entered the lock. Then the first gate was closed, and the second gate was opened, so that the ship rose or fell with the changing water level and sailed on. Modern locks still work in this way.

Upper, a modern 45,000-ton liner. Center, tanker used as a floating test bed for automated engine-room control. Lower, the nuclear-powered cargo ship Savannah.

With lock gates, people could build canals over hills, lifting vessels on "steps" of water. As sea trade grew, they cut cross-country canals to link inland cities with oceans. Using the 200-mile-long Canal du Midi, built in the reign of Louis XIV, ships could sail from the Atlantic right across France and into the Mediterranean.

By the early 1800s, canals were crisscrossing Britain, carrying barges laden with iron and coal. One pack horse, which might carry 200 pounds on its back, could haul a barge bearing 40 tons. Thus it cost less to transport goods by water than by land. To move a ton of freight in the United States might cost 100 dollars by land, but only 5 dollars by barge. But when cheaper, faster railroad transport arrived, inland canals soon lost much of their trade.

Man's inland waterways grew less important. But soon the Suez and Panama canals were to change the world. They cut through continents to link oceans.

When the canal linking the Red Sea to the Nile disappeared, many people dreamed of rebuilding it. De Lesseps opened his Suez Canal in 1869. About 400 years ago, a Portuguese seaman suggested linking the Atlantic with the Pacific by cutting a great ditch across the isthmus of Panama. In 1914 the United States opened the Panama Canal.

Though the Suez Canal is 100 miles long, it has no locks. The Panama Canal is less than half that length, but crosses high land using a series of steel lock gates. Electric locomotives tow ships through these locks.

The Suez and Panama canals have rerouted shipping lanes, cutting distances and speeding trade. To travel from New York to San Francisco by the old sea route meant sailing 15,000 miles around the inhospitable Cape Horn. By way of Panama, the voyage is little more than 5000 miles. The Suez Canal cuts the journey from England to Ceylon by 3500 miles. The opening of the Suez Canal hastened the end of sailing ships and ushered in the new age of steamships☞.

Men had always dreamed of building a ship that would move independently of wind, tide, or muscle power. A monk who lived 700 years ago knew that one day such a ship would be made. This monk, Roger Bacon, foretold that "the largest ships, with only one man guiding them, will be carried with greater velocity than if they were full of sailors."

In 1690, the French scientist Denis Papin suggested steam power might drive a boat. In 1778, the Marquis Claude de Jouffroy d'Abbans tried to make steam drive a boat propelled by "web-foot" paddles. In 1783, his 182-ton *Pyroscaphe* ("fire-ship") actually moved against a river current.

People were using practical steamships long before steam locomotives☞ regularly moved on rails. In 1791, the British *Charlotte Dundas* triumphantly hauled two 70-ton boats against a 19-miles-an-hour head wind.

An early—and unsuccessful—submarine with wooden paddles, built in 1653.

In 1803, Robert Fulton—who was later to pioneer the steamboat in the United States—launched his first successful steamboat on the river Seine in France.

River steamers soon led to ocean-going ships. Propulsion at first was by revolving oars, or paddle wheels, but clipper captains were not impressed. With their massed, billowing sails, they easily outpaced the threshing steamboats. When the first steam-powered packet boat, *Savannah*, arrived off Ireland, it made so much smoke that people thought it was on fire. Because the engines were not very powerful, it raised its paddles on the homeward trip, and relied on sails alone.

Cugnot's first steam automobile☞ used so much water that it had to be refilled every quarter of a mile. Early steamships used the water around them, but at sea the salt choked their boilers. Then, in 1834, Samuel Hall patented a way of re-using steam so that the same water would last for a whole voyage.

The paddle wheels of early steamers wasted much energy by beating the surface of the water. Two thousand years ago, Archimedes the Greek had devised a screw for raising water. In 1838, the *Archimedes*, a 237-ton screw-driven vessel, made its maiden trip. There followed a historic tug-of-war between screws and paddle wheels. The old paddle steamer *Alecto* took on the new screw-driven warship *Rattler*. The *Alecto* churned up water in a desperate fury; the *Rattler* raised scarcely a ripple, but won. Screw propellers☞ had come to stay.

Bigger and better engines, and more efficient propellers, seemed to remove all limits on the size of ships. But engineers discovered that a ship poised on the crest of a wave tended to "hog" or droop fore and aft. In a wave trough, however, it would sag in the middle. Wooden ships more than 300 feet long could not withstand such stresses and strains. Thus wooden ships were limited in size.

Shipbuilders began to put their trust in iron. They copied wooden keels and wooden ribs in iron, which was stronger than wood and was not restricted to a tree trunk's length. Scott Russell and Isambard

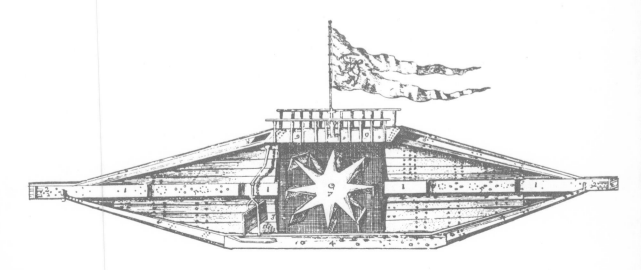

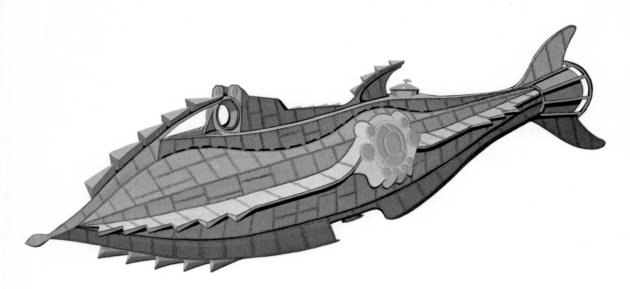

In 20,000 Leagues Under The Sea *(1869), Jules Verne imagined the submarine of the future. (Drawing from the model used in the Walt Disney film.)*

Brunel, the 19th-century English engineers, built iron ships with iron bulkhead partitions that replaced the older ribs. They built what was then the world's biggest ship.

The *Great Eastern,* as it was called, was more than 600 feet long, displaced 22,500 tons of water, was driven by two 60-foot paddle wheels, carried 6500 square yards of sail, and had the largest screw ever seen. With six masts and five funnels, it was designed to carry 4000 passengers in great luxury nonstop from England to Australia. Its 12,000-ton coal bunkers fueled 6600-horsepower engines.

The *Great Eastern* was a brave but impossible monster, and proved too costly to run. It ended its active life laying Atlantic cables, like "an elephant spinning a cobweb." Its huge coal consumption was one of the roots of its failure, and the vast engines were too weak. It was built too soon, but it left its mark; great liners descended from it.

Steam power meant that seamen no longer had to depend on a fair wind. It meant that larger ships, manned by smaller crews, could carry more goods and passengers. As the steam locomotive helped to open up new lands, so the steamship brought more people to settle those lands.

The original steamship, like the steam locomotive, burned coal or wood. On long journeys, it sometimes carried as much fuel as cargo, because its engines wasted more steam than they used. In 1854, a new invention reduced this waste by passing the steam through several cylinders in turn. Then, in 1894, Charles Parsons invented a turbine engine that could be used to power a ship. Like the lateen sail, which made better use of wind power, the marine turbine engine introduced a new age in the history of water transport.

What is a turbine? *Turbo* is the Latin name for "spinning top," or anything that spins around. Unlike piston engines, which work to and fro, turbines are engines that revolve. The windmill, for instance, is a sort of turbine. Charles Parsons' "windmill" was a set of blades fixed to a shaft. A jet of steam spun the blades around, and the shaft, revolving 3000 times every minute, spun gear wheels that turned a propeller; this in turn would drive a ship.

Parsons found that his turbine gave greater speed and power, yet used less fuel than a piston engine. At a Spithead review of the British navy in 1897, the 2000-horsepower engines of Parsons' 44-ton *Turbinia* enabled the ship to reach a speed of $34\frac{1}{2}$ knots, more than 39 land miles an hour.

By 1900, iron piston-engined ships were as obsolete as the wooden, wind-powered clippers they themselves supplanted. Light, tough steel replaced heavy iron hulls. But this took time and experiment. Bessemer's process meant that people could mass-produce steel cheaply. But, if overheated and slowly cooled, this steel was often soft and weak. The Siemens-Martin process helped to ensure a stronger, safer steel. Very soon, all shipbuilders were changing to this new material.

The U.S. submarine Nautilus, *the world's first nuclear-powered ship (1955).*

Above, the principle of hovercraft propulsion. Airstream is shown in red. Opposite, a 165-ton hovercraft of the type used between France and England.

Steel and turbines led to greater speeds, and also to bigger ships. In 1906, Britain's 32,000-ton *Mauretania* astonished the world. Its rudder alone weighed 60 tons, and the plates contained 4,000,000 rivets. Turbines of 70,000 horsepower thrust it through the seas at 27 knots. Men made still bigger ships. In 1938, the *Queen Elizabeth* appeared—the world's biggest passenger ship to date. Its turbines developed 200,000 horsepower. But the *United States*, on its 1952 maiden voyage, surpassed all liners in performance. It crossed the Atlantic in less than $3\frac{1}{2}$ days. The average speed equaled 41 land miles an hour. The best day's run—868 miles—almost doubled the record that had been set up by the fastest sailing clipper.

Modern ships are not only bigger and faster; they are safer, too. Their double hulls of steel are less easily holed. Their watertight compartments have sometimes kept a ship floating even when it was broken in two. Radar☞, the gyrocompass, and echo-sounding devices now make collisions and accidents unlikely. Modern ships are better planned as well. A century ago, European emigrants to America had to travel packed like animals in the holds. An emigrant today can travel in liners that are floating luxury hotels.

Cargo-carrying is also scientifically planned, both in packaging and in the design of the carriers. Ill-suited cargoes, indifferently stored, once wasted much space in a ship. People loaded oil in thousands of casks, piled separately in an ordinary hold. Today, oil is piped straight into the ship, into bulkheads☞ that are giant tanks. Tankers☞, strengthened by bulkheads, are the largest ships afloat; 300,000-tonners are already carrying the fuel on which our age depends—fuel for our diesel engines☞, turbines, aircraft☞, factories, and automobiles.

What is the future of ocean transport? The sea around us will always be an international highway. But there will be new uses and new shapes for tomorrow's ships. Though ocean liners are unlikely to increase in size, they will certainly increase in efficiency. The new *Queen Elizabeth 2*, a 58,000-ton liner, is designed to carry as many passengers as the old *Queen Elizabeth*, at the same cruising speed, but at only half the fuel consumption.

Underwater craft have existed for years in the shape of armed submarines☞. But atomic science now enables us to send a nuclear-powered submarine vast distances under water, even under the Arctic ice cap, without surfacing or refueling. A small supply of uranium can provide a nuclear submarine with enough energy for a voyage lasting several years.

Today, ships also travel above the surface of the water. One such invention, the *hydrofoil*☞, lifts a vessel out of the waves on stilts based on submarine wings. Another overwater "ship" is the *hovercraft*☞, a kind of aquatic flying saucer that skims over the water on a cushion of compressed air. The cushion is provided by a series of jets that force air onto the water below. Britain's pioneer hovercraft weighed $3\frac{1}{2}$ tons, and could move along at 25 knots. Now, giant hovercraft act as cross-Channel ferries, carrying 600 passengers at a time, at more than twice the speed of a conventional ferry boat.

Little by little, man has learned better ways of crossing the once impassable oceans. He has plans for still better ships. But the new nuclear-powered craft have already introduced a new age of sea power. In time, sail, steam, and even the powerful oil turbine, will seem almost as primitive as the Stone-Age dugout canoe.

4 Man Explores the Air

Today, man's speed increases as he moves from water to land, and from land to air. By 1967, the American Lee Taylor had set a world water speed record of 285 miles an hour. On land, Lieutenant-Colonel John P. Stapp, in New Mexico, had reached 632 miles an hour in an experimental rocket☞ sled. In the air, William J. Knight had piloted his X-15 rocket plane over California at 4534 miles an hour.

It is above the surface of the ground that man moves fastest. Yet it was only recently that he took his first tentative toe-dip in the boundless ocean of the sky. For most of its first quarter of a million years, mankind remained stolidly earthbound.

Yet one of man's oldest dreams was to escape from the earth, to break free from the fetters of gravity, and to soar like a bird over mountain barriers or skim over the ocean waves. These dreams survive in ancient legends of winged horses and magic carpets, and of the Greek boy Icarus, who fixed feathered wings to his arms and crashed to his death in the sea.

But feathered birds have, weight for weight, much stronger shoulder muscles than man. Ignorant of this, and of the other reasons why birds can fly, people turned wishful fantasy into unscientific experiment. History is littered with the broken bodies of "birdmen" who leaped to their death from towers.

By A.D. 1700, people were making fresh experiments, using lighter-than-air balloons☞. In 1782, the Montgolfier brothers succeeded in raising a hot-air balloon. Bulk for bulk, hot air is lighter than cold air, and that is why their hot-air balloon went up.

Air is a mixture of several gases, some heavier, some lighter than the whole. In 1783, Professor J. A. Charles succeeded in manufacturing hydrogen, a lighter-than-air gas. He filled a silk balloon with it. The balloon floated upward through the denser air as a rubber ball floats through water. Balloons were the vessels in which man first explored the skies above him.

Hot-air balloon with sails, designed by the Montgolfier brothers in 1785.

The first balloonists could rise and fly through the air, but they were unable to steer their craft. They could partly control their rise and fall by adjusting ballast and supplies of gas. But otherwise they were merely drifters, at the mercy of wind and air currents.

In the 19th century, people began to study afresh the way birds fly and steer themselves. People knew that the albatross, the eagle, and the buzzard could glide and soar effortlessly, with scarcely a flap of their wings. These birds gave inventors the idea of building heavier-than-air gliding machines with fixed, rather than flapping, wings.

The greatest of the 19th-century gliding experts was Otto Lilienthal, born in 1848. This German pioneer built an artificial hill near Berlin. From it, he made thousands of short flights in gliders. He was attempting to discover the birds' natural secret: how to use air itself to keep a body airborne and to propel it forward. Today we call this science *aerodynamics* ☞ (the study of gases moving over an object).

We have seen already that air is a mixture of molecules of many gases, including oxygen, nitrogen, hydrogen, and others. Molecules are too small to be visible. We can feel them resist a sheet of cardboard if we wave it in the air, yet there is almost no resistance if we hold the cardboard flat and move it edgewise through the air.

Lilienthal, taking his tip from the birds, shaped his wings so that air resistance would give them lift, but streamlined them so that air resistance scarcely held them back. Modern aircraft ☞ wings still work in this way. Held level with the ground, a wing will not lift. But if its leading edge is uptilted slightly, the air crammed beneath the wing thrusts it upward. In flight, the leading edge cleaves the air in two airstreams, one flowing over, and one under, the wing. The two streams close up after the wing has passed.

Many wings are designed in a flowing curve, concave beneath, and convex above. Thus the upper airstream must move faster than the lower one, for it has farther to travel. But air is elastic. The fast-moving particles of the upper airstream get widely separated, creating a partial vacuum that sucks the wing upward. Two thirds of the lift of a modern aircraft may be due to this suction.

Lilienthal learned much from his many glides. He learned how to balance his machine in a wind, in order to keep it straight and level. Thanks to improvements in photography, experts the world over could study the details of Lilienthal's gliders. But that great pioneer lost his life gliding when the wind suddenly dropped. Without a powered aircraft, he was unable to gain speed quickly enough to create sufficient lift for his wings.

The glider was the pathfinder for modern aircraft. But not until man had devised a powered, heavier-than-air machine could he claim to have conquered the air. Steam engines ☞ had made man's ships

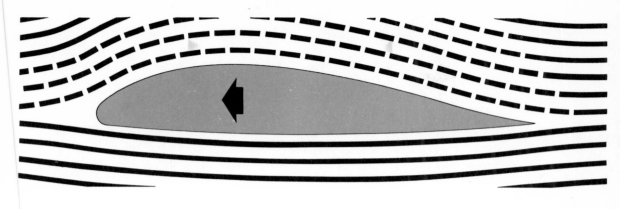

Above, cross section through the wing of an aircraft, showing how it splits the airstream into two.

Left, Otto Lilienthal flying one of his gliders in 1890. He controlled the machine by shifting the weight of his body against the wind.

Below, the Flyer, *the machine with which the Wrights made the first successful powered flight (1903).*

independent of the wind. But steam engines were too unwieldy to put into gliders. People needed something lighter and more powerful. The solution to their problem was an engine that changed the world.

The brothers Orville and Wilbur Wright had long been experimenting with gliders. From others' earlier experiments and the way the Wrights warped their glider's wings (flexible like those of a soaring bird) came the invention of ailerons☞. Ailerons control the banked turn of a modern aircraft. But the Wrights still had to design a plane that could successfully carry its own power. They took a 12-horsepower version of the new, compact, internal-combustion engine☞ and fitted it in an airframe.

At 10.30 A.M. on December 17, 1903, at Kitty Hawk, North Carolina, Orville Wright, watched by his brother Wilbur, took his screw-driven box crate into the air and flew for 40 yards. The flight was short, lasting only 12 seconds. They were the most momentous 12 seconds in the history of flight.

The Wright brothers had achieved the first powered flight, and their success inspired other enthusiasts. With aircraft as flimsy as chicken coops, people flung themselves into the sky. The next few years were a time of crazy adventure.

Soon a British newspaper, the *Daily Mail*, offered £1000 to the first aviator to fly a plane across the English Channel. Early in the morning of July 25, 1909, Louis Blériot, a Frenchman, wheeled his frail-looking monoplane, made of glued wood and sailcloth, down to the shore near Calais. At 4.35 A.M. he climbed into the cockpit, revved the 25-horsepower engine, took off, and headed out to sea. Exactly 35 minutes and 30 seconds later, he landed on English soil. Blériot won the £1000 prize, but he did more than that. He showed that flying machines defied all boundaries.

In 1913, the *Daily Mail* offered a new prize of £10,000 for a nonstop flight across the North Atlantic, but World War I delayed the attempt. In 1919, a converted bomber, piloted by two World War veterans, Alcock and Brown, set out on the great adventure.

Weighed down with fuel for its almost 2000-mile flight, their six-ton Vickers *Vimy* biplane, powered by 700-horsepower engines, lumbered across a Newfoundland field and climbed heavily over the sea.

Blériot had lost his way; but that mattered little in a flight of some 30 miles. Alcock and Brown were flying more than 60 times that distance without a single landmark to guide them. Brown worked out the navigation☞ using an ordinary Mercator map and a naval sextant to check position.

Their journey was groping, blind, and perilous. The plane soon ran into fog. Such blind-flying instruments as they had were poor. Their radio transmitter failed. Fog and cloud obscured the sun by day and the

McDonnell F4C Phantom 1968

Spad XIII 1918

On this page we compare a present-day fighting plane, the Phantom F-4C *jet, to a fighter of World War I, the* Spad XIII.

Pilots

Armament

Grenade   Gun

Missiles   Bomb

Speed

Take-off

Above, the F-4C *climbs to its ceiling height of 98,000 feet in only 6 minutes 11 seconds; the old* Spad XIII *took 4 minutes 6 seconds to reach 6500 feet.*

stars for much of the night. The airmen flew through a waste of mists over trackless, silent sea.

But worse was to come. A towering mass of storm-cloud rose up to bar their way. Within it lurked lightning, and raging up-currents that could crumple their bomber like a leaf. Turbulent eddies in the gale-force winds began to batter the plane. The airspeed indicator failed. The plane lost speed and began to spiral seaward in a long and treacherous spin. Alcock regained control at the last moment and pulled the plane up from the waves. He climbed, but, in the cold of the upper air, ice began forming on the wings and engine. Brown had to clamber out on the wings and hack off the ice with a knife. He was forced to do this many times before the welcome shores of Ireland appeared. Alcock and Brown upended in a bog. But they had made history by flying the Atlantic.

Other pioneer flights followed quickly. In the same year, Keith and Ross Smith flew from England to Australia in less than 30 days. In 1924, two U.S. seaplanes☞ flew more than 27,000 miles around the world. In 1927, Charles Lindbergh flew solo in a single-engined monoplane from New York to Paris. His nonstop route was nearly double the length of that taken by Alcock and Brown.

Those early airmen showed a new kind of courage. They opened skyways where no men had been. They flew with few guiding instruments, some in planes as flimsy as cardboard. Many of them lost their lives. But this small band of adventurers, often alone, pioneered the air routes we travel today. They spun the first slender strands of the commercial airlines that have now become a worldwide web.

The history of powered flight is little more than half a century old, yet already man is reaching into space. This amazing advance would have been less rapid had it not been for two world wars. Each created conditions of desperate rivalry that forced designers into new ideas.

In 1914, there was only one kind of plane in the air. By 1918, the war had produced specialized aircraft of many kinds: spotters, trainers, transports, seaplanes, light fighters, and heavy bombers.

The first warplanes were simply scouts. They flew over enemy lines to spot the movements of troops or to direct the shelling of targets invisible from the ground. Sometimes a pilot took a pistol with him and swapped shots with enemy scouts in the air.

Then a Dutchman, Fokker, invented a fixed machine gun synchronized to fire through a spinning propeller☞. Mounted in front of the cockpit, it was fired by the pilot, who aimed both his plane and his gun at the target. It changed the plane into a lethal weapon and was the beginning of war in the air.

In this strange new combat, fighter pilots circled each other, turning in ever tightening curves trying to bring their fixed guns to bear. The

Four types of jet engine, and aircraft or missiles in which they are used.

Ram-jet

Nord Griffon fighter.

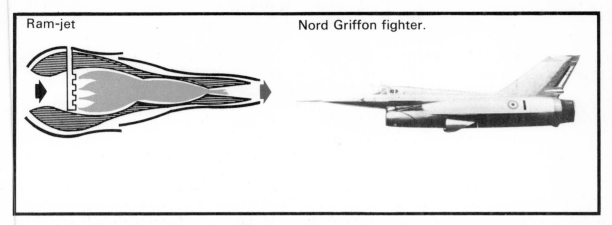

Pulse-jet

V.1. flying bomb

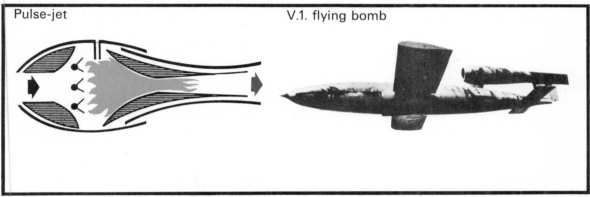

Turbo-prop

Vickers Vanguard airliner

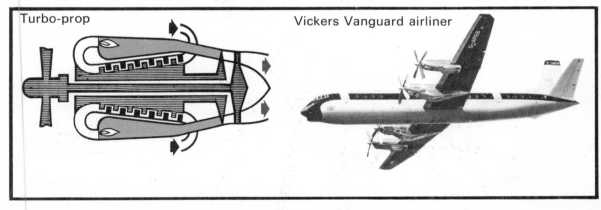

Turbo-jet

Boeing 707 jet liner

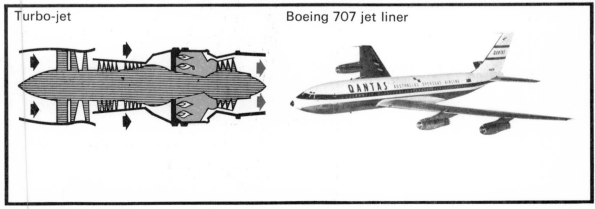

plane that could turn in the tightest circle, or climb the fastest, was very often the victor. This was a spur to aircraft designers to make planes more powerful and more maneuverable.

The aerobatics of the air war provided valuable tests for pilots as well as planes. Ace pilots, such as the German Immelmann, mastered tactics such as the "falling leaf" and the spin. The school of war produced the pilots who were to become the great fliers of the post-war years.

The fighters developed during World War I led to faster, higher-flying planes. Aircraft in 1914 averaged 75 miles an hour and seldom climbed to more than 10,000 feet. Four years later, fighters were flying at twice that speed and more than twice that height. Engineers had developed bombers that could fly great distances and carry great loads. Germany built Gothas to bomb the city of London. Britain built Handley Pages to bomb Berlin. Heavy bombers led to the first long-distance airliners.

In 1914, Britain had about 300 warplanes. By 1918, the number had increased to 20,000. By then, people were mass-producing planes from standard parts, but aircraft were still cluttered up by struts and wires,

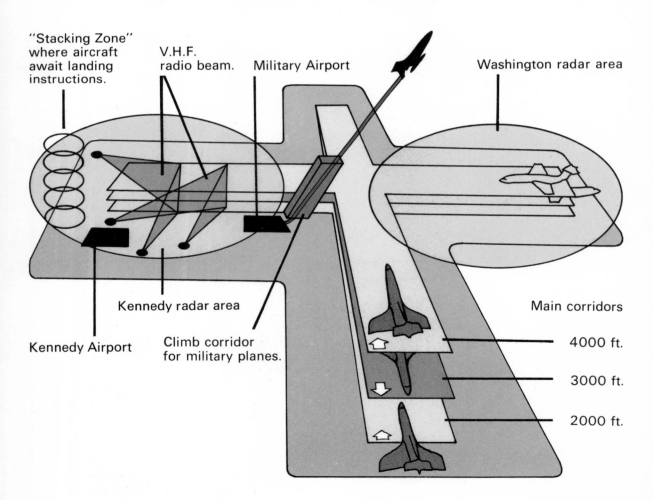

"Stacking Zone" where aircraft await landing instructions.

V.H.F. radio beam.

Military Airport

Washington radar area

Kennedy radar area

Kennedy Airport

Climb corridor for military planes.

Main corridors

4000 ft.

3000 ft.

2000 ft.

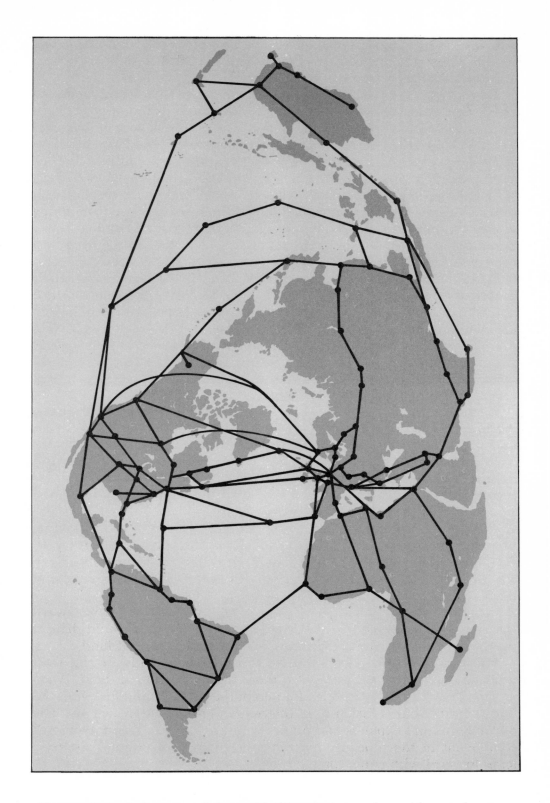

Above, principal air routes of the world. Opposite page, air corridors, radar zones, and radio zones that guide a pilot on a New York-Washington flight.

which hampered their speed in the air. Nevertheless, aircraft engines had developed more than twice their prewar horsepower without a corresponding increase in weight.

Twenty years of peace produced a few advances. Designers replaced thin fabric coverings with skins of light alloy metals, and open cockpits became closed-in cabins. International air races, such as the Schneider Trophy, led to the development of the monoplane, whose wings, weight for weight, gave greater lift than those of wartime biplanes.

The six feverish years of World War II again changed the face of the sky. They produced planes such as the world had never seen, and in tens of thousands. These included streamlined fighters, pilotless flying bombs, troop carriers, tank and gun transports, long-range heavy bombers—such as the four-engined B-29—helicopters☞, and at last the jet.

World War II pushed the speed of the propeller-driven aircraft to its practical limit. In 1939, a German Messerschmidt fighter had reached a speed of 469 miles an hour. By 1945, no propeller-driven piston-engined aircraft was able to fly much faster. One reason is that a propeller cannot cope with turbulent air currents set up at high speeds.

But wartime engineers were already seeking new ways to make aircraft travel faster and higher. For some years, they had been experimenting with jet propulsion☞. This solved their problem.

What is jet propulsion? In principle, it is really nothing new. Propeller-driven planes are, in fact, jet-propelled. A propeller not only thrusts air backward, but also moves forward itself with a reaction equal to the backward thrust of the air. Sir Isaac Newton worked out how this happens, long before the propeller-driven plane had been invented. He proved that "action and reaction are equal in magnitude and opposite in direction."

You can prove this yourself by diving off the stern of a free-floating boat. You go one way, and thrust the boat in the opposite direction. In swimming, you move forward by pushing water backward. So it is in the air. One can move through it only by using this same principle of reaction.

Inventors found that a jet of gases could give a greater backward thrust than a propeller. So they made a jet engine that would drive a plane. How does it work? Scientists have invented several kinds.

The ramjet is just a hollow tube, open at both ends. It can start working only when it is moving at more than 300 miles an hour. Then its speed rams air into the open funnels of the tube. Liquid fuel, injected into the tube, burns furiously in the oxygen of the compressed air. The burning mixture expands and pushes with great force against a forward component in the tube. By reaction, the plane built around the tube leaps forward with equal force.

Pulse-jets, on the other hand, are ramjets with inlet valves that open and shut so that the air pulses through the tube instead of flowing in a steady stream. Both ramjets and pulse-jets need special high-speed launching methods.

The jets we most often see today are turbojets and turboprops. Turbojet planes, unlike ramjets, can take off unaided. A compressor fan inside the jet tube sucks in air at the speed that the ramjet normally needs before it can start to work. Compressed air passes to combustion chambers, where it mixes with injected fuel. A spark ignites the mixture, and it expands, as before, to thrust the aircraft forward. As it escapes from the combustion chambers, the expanding gas turns a set of turbine blades fixed to a shaft. The shaft itself spins the compression fan. The fan sucks in more air, and the cycle is repeated.

A turboprop works like a turbojet. But the shaft that links the turbine and compressor extends farther and ends in a propeller. Thus the gases in a turboprop are used to turn three "windmills" instead of two: turbine, compressor, *and* propeller.

Many people first learned of jet propulsion when they saw and heard British turbojet *Gloster* fighters chasing German pulse-jet flying bombs.

A short- and medium-distance freight plane, with a capacity of up to 16 tons.

But it is only since World War II that we have really learned what ramjets, pulse-jets, turbojets, and turboprops can do.

Jet-powered planes are now the kings of the sky and are cutting flying times dramatically. But for profitable peacetime uses, airline designers had to make a choice between them. Military ramjets and pulse-jets were too costly to run. A jet was needed that would run cheaper, as well as faster, than piston-engined planes.

A piston engine can develop one horsepower for each pound it weighs. Some turbines developed the same power for half the weight. Lighter engines meant that an aircraft could carry a bigger payload. The Vickers *Vanguard* airliner was planned to reduce air fares by half.

Turbojets (now available with quieter, more economical fan engines) and turboprops have turned the transatlantic skyway, pioneered by Alcock and Brown, into a routine trip for thousands. The pioneers flew nonstop from Newfoundland to Ireland, 1890 miles, in 16 hours. The first Atlantic jet liner, the *Comet*, flew nonstop from New York to London, 3000 miles, in under 8 hours.

The first two men to fly the Atlantic sat cramped in a half-open cockpit. In the giant turbofan airliner of today, you take your place

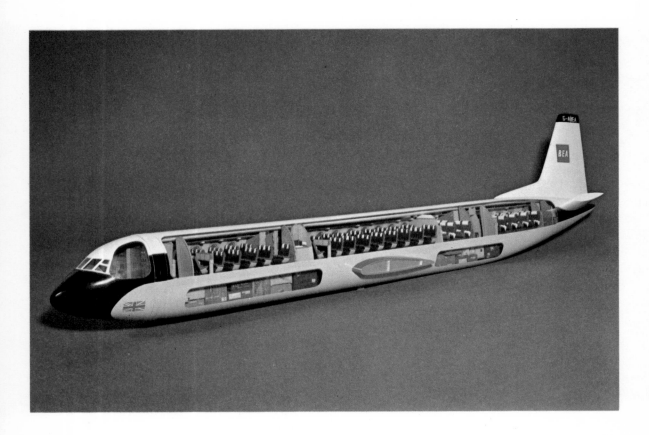

Cutaway model of a Vickers Vanguard *airliner, with a seating capacity of 110.*

with 138 other passengers in a cabin as comfortable as a hotel lounge. Then a skilled team—pilot, copilot, third pilot, and flight engineer—takes over. In a *Super VC10*, the pilot unleashes a thrust of 21,800 pounds from four great turbofans at the rear of the fuselage☞.

At first, the plane climbs steeply into the sky, then levels out, well over six miles up. You are now flying far higher than the highest mountain, above the turbulent winds and storms, at a speed of about nine miles a minute. The thin air offers your jet liner little resistance.

One of the stewardesses brings you a hot meal from the galley. Another brings you notepaper if you wish to write—and you can write with ease. The smooth-working jets, using a gallon of fuel every two seconds, banish the vibration of piston engines.

Snug in your warm luxurious cabin, you have no sensation of the height at which you are traveling. Air pressure outside is about four times less than at sea level, and the air is far too thin for you to breathe; but you are racing through it in a safely sealed pressurized capsule. Air temperature outside is about $-15°C$; but a regulated flow of warmed and moistened air, tapped from the compressors in the turbojets, feeds you the oxygen you need.

Servicing and restocking a Boeing *airliner at* London *airport before a flight.*

Top, Paul Cornu's helicopter (1907). Center, the rotodyne, the world's first vertical takeoff airliner. Lower, military helicopters dropping troops.

At first, people feared that jet liners would prove too costly. It is true that their thirst for fuel is huge. The old-fashioned airliner certainly used far less. Yet at nine miles a minute, the jet liner spends far less time in the air.

New subsonic jet liners include the giant *Boeing 747* or "jumbo jet" ☞ ; powered by four turbofan engines, it is designed to carry up to 490 people at a speed of 625 miles an hour. But the most exciting developments are the new airliners in the supersonic range, such as the Anglo-French *Concorde*, and the Russian *Tupolev Tu-144*. Both are designed for cruising speeds of about 1450 miles an hour, the *Concorde* using turbojet engines and the *Tu-144* turbofans. The *Boeing SST*, an even more ambitious design, will use the swing-wing, or variable geometry, concept, at supersonic speeds. Though many problems of supersonic flight ☞ remain to be solved, the supersonic airliner may eventually become as commonplace as the subsonic airliner of today.

Can you hear an aircraft at this moment? It is more than likely that you can. Every second of the day, an aircraft is taking off or landing somewhere in the world. Modern skies are a web of invisible roads, along which airliners are continually passing. They fly over 170,000 million miles a year, equal to more than 750 trips to the sun.

Aircraft are changing the map of the world. The map that most of us know was designed by Mercator more than 400 years ago. And he made it for sailors, not for airmen. His projection shows us the round globe pressed flat, and this is done by stretching the polar regions to enormous width. Mercator's maps also show Canada and Siberia at opposite ends of the earth; by polar air routes, they are, in fact, near neighbors. You can fly from London to Tokyo by way of Moscow and Peking, by a great circle route that is over 1000 miles shorter than the route through India.

Great circle routes are the shortest routes between any two points on the globe. But, for practical reasons, most commercial aircraft do not use them. They must zigzag across the globe to serve cities that were built long before air routes were established.

Just as the captains of sailing ships followed predictable winds, so jet pilots today take advantage of fast airstreams that flow at 30,000 feet.

What kind of cargoes do aircraft carry? People, of course, are the chief "cargo." Speed is the aircraft's chief advantage. The need for speed determines the kinds of freight that aircraft carry—for example, urgently needed mail, drugs, and blood plasma.

Some airlines have special planes for special jobs. There are freight planes, for instance, that can carry quite heavy loads—some, up to 40 tons. In the Antarctic, aircraft helped to set up an American base at the South Pole. In sub-arctic Canada, freighters flew in much of the material that went to build Uranium City.

Many isolated regions depend on planes. Planes in turn depend on airports☞, the springboards of modern travel. A century ago, barren islands became important coaling stations for steamships☞. Today, the needs of the air routes are putting other remote places on the map. In Newfoundland, Greenland, Hawaii, and the Azores, places that were once small villages are now major junctions of the air.

A modern airport should be sited near sea level, where denser air gives an aircraft's wings the greatest lift. It should also be free from fog. A jet liner needs a well-surfaced two-mile-long runway, and each airport must have several runways facing different ways, because planes take off and land into the wind. Airports must have many buildings to service planes, control traffic, store cargo, house airline staff, and shelter passengers.

All these needs pose problems, especially near cities. The greatest problem of all is space. The jet liners need great runways, but open land near cities is scarce. City smoke may also create smog that blacks out the city's airport. How shall we solve these problems of the air age?

Like the sea, the air can be wild. Blériot had to wait for a fair wind before he could fly the Channel. Today, thanks to modern machines and safety devices, airliners fly in almost any weather.

If you are a pilot about to take a trip, you must tell your airport authority where you intend to go. The airport staff pass this information on to airports along your route. But first they give you the weather news, very often radioed from ships or weather stations hundreds of miles away. Armed with this information, you can plot your course, allowing for winds, and can even plan to dodge a storm as much as a thousand miles away.

At airports that handle over a thousand planes a day, the skies and runways may be crowded. Before you take off, therefore, traffic controllers scan radar☞ screens to ensure that runway and sky are clear.

Once you are in the air, radio beams from the airports lead you safely along an invisible corridor through the sky. Nowadays, many pilots fly the whole of their journey along radio beams.

If the flight is long and straight, you may set your controls in such a way that the aircraft flies itself. Engineers have learned to link a gyroscope (a special compass) with motors that automatically work the control surfaces of the plane and keep it on course. Controlled by automatic pilot☞ alone, planes have flown from America to Britain.

You have many devices to ensure the safety of your plane: navigation lights blink from wing tips and tail, automatic dials record airspeed and height, an artificial horizon shows if you are flying level, and indicators show your rate of fuel consumption.

Many of these instruments are like the senses that keep our bodies informed of what is going on around us. Without a central brain to

Center, models of the Boeing SST, *showing its two alternative wing positions. Lower, the Anglo-French* Concorde, *designed to fly at twice the speed of sound.*

Above, how shock waves form around an aircraft traveling at supersonic speeds.

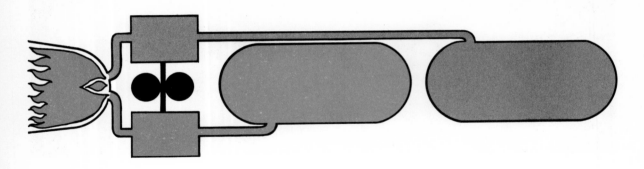

A liquid-fuel rocket motor. Fuel and oxidant are pumped into the combustion chamber, where fuel burns in oxidant, providing the thrust that lifts rocket.

control them, they are useless. Unlike the automatic pilot, you are trained to react instantly to emergencies, which a machine cannot always sense. The quiver of a needle on a dial may mean that you have no more than a few seconds to switch off a faulty engine.

At your journey's end, you may find other planes landing in front of you. Ground control will then direct you to an invisible "siding" in the air. There you can circle safely until you get permission to land. Low cloud may hide the runway, but ground control can see you by radar and will be able to "talk you down." Even if fog blots out the airport completely, bringing all normal movements to a halt, your aircraft may be able to make a safe landing under automatic control. At last you taxi safely down the runway. You have flown thousands of miles, aided by devices that make air travel safer than a road trip.

One of the problems we face in our age of jet liners is the great space these aircraft require—a two-mile runway for takeoff and landing. Because of this space problem, most big airports are built on the outskirts of cities. Kennedy Airport is 16 miles from Manhattan, and London Airport is 14 miles from the city center. It takes almost as long to get from London to its airport as it takes to fly from that airport to Paris.

Many people see the answer to this problem in aircraft that can take off and land straight up and down. The helicopter, which can rise from and land on a roof top, was the first successful experiment in this direction. People already use it as a link between some cities and their airports, turning an hour's crawl into a 10-minute hop.

Like most inventions, helicopters were first thought of many hundreds of years ago. Leonardo da Vinci drew a sketch for one in about the year 1500. But no one could make one work until recent times. The first manned helicopter flight on record was made in 1907, by Louis and Jacques Breguet of France.

By 1940, Igor Sikorsky had overcome the delicate problem of keeping the craft properly balanced in the air. Sikorsky's helicopters have no wings. A set of huge rotor blades mounted on a vertical shaft lifts the machine straight up in the air. The blades are especially angled to give the craft lift, rather like a set of wings spinning round and round. When the pilot wants to climb, he steepens the angle of the blades, so that they increase lift by biting harder into the air. To hover, he lessens the angle; and to move forward, he tilts the rotor shaft slightly so that the blades tilt forward too. To prevent the fuselage swinging with the turn of the rotor, Sikorsky built a small propeller facing sideways on the tail. It acted as a stabilizer as well as a rudder.

In 1941, Sikorsky made the first helicopter flight of more than a hundred minutes. Since then, helicopters have flown many thousands of miles, and have also saved many thousands of lives during rescue work. People have used them for lifting trucks☞, ferrying mail to ships and islands, stringing power lines across the Rockies, and rescuing injured mountain climbers, shipwreck victims, and wounded soldiers.

Many helicopters can carry up to 30 passengers at 150 miles an hour for several hundred miles. But helicopters at their present stage have not the speed or range of long-distance airliners.

To make a "heliliner," it seems that we need an aircraft that rises like a helicopter, then flies like an ordinary plane. Aircraft companies all over the world are working on projects for fast "convertiplanes" that would have both foldaway rotor blades for takeoff and fixed wings for ordinary flight.

We already have small jet aircraft capable of making a vertical or short-distance takeoff and landing—such as the Hawker Siddeley *Harrier*, a fighter that was designed to operate from 500-yard strips. Now inventors are experimenting with jets that will enable an airliner to make a vertical takeoff☞ and landing, to save power and the space wasted by two-mile runways. Such an invention would greatly increase the speed of air transportation.

How is a new type of aircraft born? An early aviator could plan, build, and fly his own machine. Today, large teams of experts must combine on each new project. Imagine that you are the chairman of an aircraft company. Your government has asked you to build an entirely new plane. The plane must fly faster than any plane in use today, yet carry a large number of passengers. How do you set about it?

First, you tell the people in your project design office exactly what you want. They will make some basic drawings of the idea. After careful consultation, you choose the one that seems best. Designers then make thousands of exact drawings, showing every detail of the plane. These drawings may involve thousands of mathematical calculations and thousands of experiments with models.

You have to build a plane that will work as well in the stratosphere, where air pressure, temperature, and lift are low, as it will at sea level, where these are high. From ground to stratosphere, your plane must often pass through fierce changes of wind and through regions where thick ice may form on its wings. Your plane must be able to make a vertical takeoff and landing, and to cruise faster than sound.

To withstand the violent strains it is likely to meet, you may give your plane a frame of metal ribs, covered with a streamlined metal skin. New metals such as titanium are just as strong as steel, but only about half the weight, and they melt at much higher temperatures. You may also make use of new, lightweight plastics.

If you fly in thin stratospheric air, you encounter less friction. Yet at great heights you reach the sound barrier sooner. Traveling at the speed of sound (about 760 miles an hour at sea level), an aircraft catches up with a wall of compressed air that has been driven ahead by the aircraft's movement. The air ahead has no time to divide and let the plane smoothly through, so a shock front builds up around the aircraft's nose. Thus a supersonic flight could provide as bumpy a ride as a toboggan run down a rocky hillside.

To solve this problem, aerodynamics☞ experts make many involved calculations. On the result of these, other experts build streamlined model planes with wings designed to offer little resistance to the atmosphere. You then test these models in wind tunnels, where airstreams are equivalent to supersonic flight speeds.

When you have planned the shape of your aircraft, you start to make its parts. Machines compress and stretch them, imitating the strains and stresses they must undergo in flight. When all tests are completed, your planners and engineers produce a full-scale prototype that flies. But before passengers can travel in it, the government ensures that it meets certain safety standards.

At last your new aircraft makes its maiden trip. It has greater strength than a subsonic jet liner, yet is only half its weight per passenger. It will take off and land straight up and down on air cushions created by its jets. Its landing strip need be no bigger than an ordinary car park. To avoid the friction set up in dense air at low levels, it may fly as high as 40 miles up. Heat tapped from the jets will keep the plane free from ice. It will carry over 200 passengers at 15 times the speed of sound, making New York to London a half-hour trip.

Today, aircraft exist that can carry a man around the earth in a day. Yet man is still not satisfied. Already he looks out from his shrinking home planet to the moon and other planets. What secrets do they hold? Man will not rest until he knows.

But how can man escape the Earth? To overcome gravity, he must travel at 25,000 miles an hour. What machine could help him make

Opposite: diagram (left) shows the Saturn *rocket that has carried men to the moon: drawings show three stages of a journey to the moon and back.*

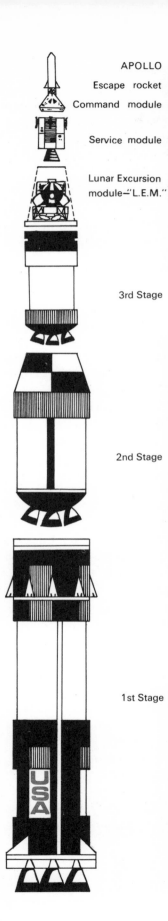

APOLLO

Escape rocket

Command module

Service module

Lunar Excursion
module–"L.E.M."

3rd Stage

2nd Stage

1st Stage

Above, from earth orbit the space craft is launched toward the moon. Below, the lunar vehicle lands on the moon.

UNITED STATES

The lunar vehicle rejoins the parent craft, which, when the landing crew is aboard, sets off back to earth (below).

such a leap? The most powerful jet planes would be no use. At about 50,000 feet, most jets peter out. In the thin upper atmosphere, there is no oxygen at all. Steam engines, internal-combustion engines, and jets, the machines that help man move on earth, depend on oxygen within the earth's atmosphere.

Strangely enough, one of the answers to this problem has been in the hands of children for years. The rocket, even a toy one, is a flying machine that burns fuel independently of oxygen in the atmosphere. The Chinese invented rockets more than 1000 years ago. They packed charcoal, sulfur, and saltpeter in a tube, and tied it to an arrow. When the rocket was fired, expanding gases rushed from the tube and sped the arrow on its way. In 1232, "flying fire arrows" terrified Mongol invaders.

The Chinese could not have known the future importance of their discovery; and they were ignorant that the fuel they used burned without the help of air. In fact, saltpeter, when heated, breaks down into oxygen, which mixes with the other chemicals in gunpowder and makes them burn.

The Chinese rocket was propelled by "equal and opposite reaction." Reaction rockets work even better in a vacuum than in air, which slows them down. Given enough force to pierce the earth's atmosphere, rockets fly best in airless space itself.

In time, Chinese gunpowder rockets were used in India and Europe. But by 1900 most armies used gunpowder only to fire bullets and shells. Yet some far-sighted people saw strange new possibilities for the rocket. In 1903, the Russian Konstantin Tsiolkovsky published an article called "Exploration of Space with Reaction Instruments." He believed that rockets could reach the moon. But he knew that concentrated liquid fuel must replace gunpowder to produce enough power and speed. Robert Goddard in America and Hermann Oberth in Germany also pioneered the rocket age.

In 1942, on the Baltic island of Peenemünde, a group of German scientists anxiously watched a giant rocket that stood upended on the ground. Suddenly a great burst of flame surrounded its base. The 14-ton monster rose slowly from its pad, reacting to an 8-ton thrust from its engine. It seemed to hang nearly motionless for seconds, then it picked up speed. Its thrust increased to 25 tons. The rocket accelerated and flamed out of sight. In a single minute, its motors consumed 10 tons of liquid oxygen and alcohol. Having pushed it to a speed of 3500 miles an hour, the motors cut out. The rocket began to curve in a giant arc, pulled earthward by gravity. Five minutes after launching, the V2 hit the ground, 125 miles away.

The V2s delivered destruction in their warheads. Today, rocket nose cones☞ gather information for scientists. The V2s returned to earth in

An experimental "moon tractor"—a mobile base for post-Apollo astronauts—with flexible metal wheels for negotiating the rough surface of the moon.

a few minutes. Today, some rockets can escape from earth and will cruise on through space for millions of years.

On October 4, 1957, Russia launched the first artificial earth satellite☞. A giant three-stage rocket carried the tiny globe aloft and put it into orbit around the earth. From the edge of space, it sent back startling information to man.

The first Sputnik followed an elliptical orbit. At times, it would be 560 miles away from the earth, then it would swing to within 125 miles. Each time it reentered the outer layers of our atmosphere, air friction slowed it down a little. (By measuring the changing speeds of artificial satellites, scientists are learning more about the earth's true shape. Scientists also use artificial satellites as television relay stations, and world weather stations.)

The first Sputnik broadcast information by a series of radio signals, or "bleeps." The tiny changes in these signals, recorded by sensitive apparatus on earth, helped to show changes in the minute electrically charged particles of the ionosphere. This upper region of our atmosphere plays an important part in radio transmissions. Satellites may teach us why.

Changing bleeps also told of changing atmospheric pressure and temperature inside the Sputnik's small aluminum globe. A supply of nitrogen, circulating inside, helped to control temperatures and to keep the satellite's instruments working properly. Without the nitrogen, the Sputnik's temperature would have varied by 200°C every 90 minutes as it passed from sunlight into the earth's cold shadow.

The second artificial satellite entered orbit on November 3, 1957. It was also launched by Russia. Its instruments recorded shortwave ultraviolet and X-ray radiations from the sun. These rays are damped down by the earth's atmosphere before they reach us. But, to spacemen, radiation could be dangerous. A sort of Geiger counter in *Sputnik II* measured the mysterious cosmic rays, perhaps the greatest of all radiation hazards. (They can penetrate 3000 feet of water.)

But the most valuable "instrument" in *Sputnik II* was Laika, a dog. A telemeter told scientists on earth how she breathed and fed, what her blood pressure was, and how her heart was working.

Since 1957, more artificial satellites (ranging in weight from pounds to tons) have been launched, by America as well as by Russia. Some have recorded bombardments by micrometeorites—the "heavenly pebbles" that vaporize when they strike our atmosphere at about 162,000 miles an hour. American Explorer satellites have revealed new space travel problems: belts of radiation 20,000 miles wide, held to our earth like iron filings around a magnet.

Two years to the day after she launched *Sputnik I*, Russia sent another satellite, *Luna III*, to photograph the far side of the moon—the side man had never seen. The result was a triumph of mathematics. Electronic brains helped scientists to plot the craft's elaborate course. They had to fire the projectile from our spinning globe, moving one way, at a distant target, moving another. They had to calculate the three-way gravitational pull of earth, moon, and sun. They had to aim the *Luna III* at the precise spot in space that the moon would pass two days later.

The plan worked perfectly; the rocket roared on its way. At times, the thrust of its motors was equal to that of the world's biggest hydroelectric power stations. The automatic instruments packed in the nose did the work of research workers, radio operators, cameramen, and laboratory assistants. Cameras photographed the moon; machines developed, fixed, and dried the film. Then it was radioed back to earth.

In the following year, 1960, the Americans for the first time recovered a satellite from space. This was *Discovery 13*, which was recovered from the sea after making 16 complete orbits of the earth. In the same year the Russians brought safely back to land their *Sputnik V*, which had carried two dogs, Belka and Strelka, 18 times around the earth.

The time had come for man himself to venture into space. It had been demonstrated that rockets were now powerful enough and controllable enough to put him there. It had been demonstrated that an animal could live and stay healthy in space. It had been demonstrated that a space vehicle could return safely to earth at the end of its journey. Manned space flight was a practical possibility.

The first man in space was Yuri Gagarin, a 27-year-old major in the Russian air force. On April 12, 1961, he lifted off from the launching

To survive in space, men need protective clothing such as this Apollo spacesuit.

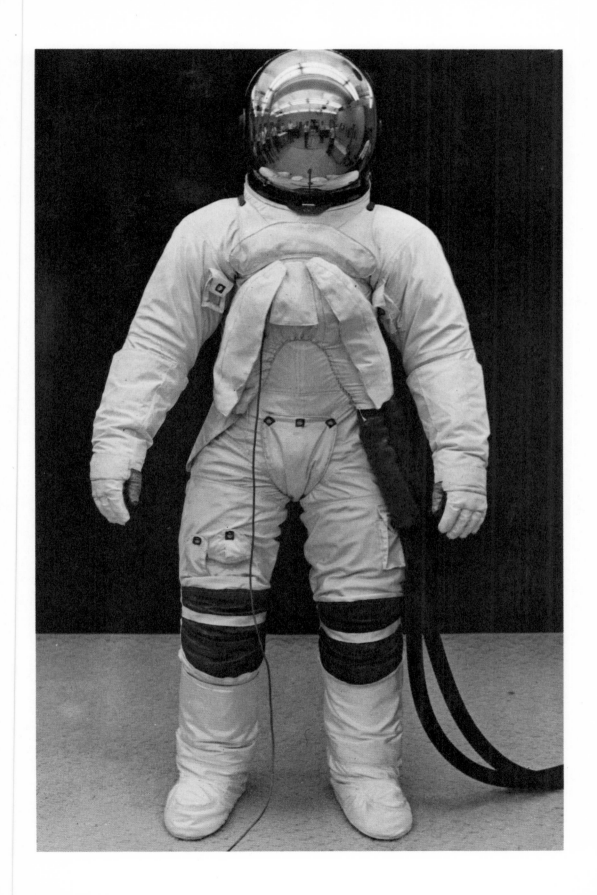

pad in *Vostok I* at 9.07 P.M., Moscow time. He landed safely one hour and 48 minutes later, having made one orbit of the earth and a pioneering journey that made history.

Less than a month later, on May 5, 1961, the United States achieved a simpler, but comparable, success when Alan B. Shepard was launched on a successful 302-mile sub-orbital shot over the Atlantic in the capsule *Freedom 7*. On August 6, the Russian astronaut Gherman Titov successfully completed 17 orbits of the earth in another *Vostok* space craft. And on February 20, 1962, came America's first manned orbital flight. John Glenn, in *Friendship 7*, completed three earth orbits in a flight time of 4 hours 55 minutes.

Glenn's space flight was important not simply because it was an American "first." There was another factor. A fault developed in the automatic steering controls while the craft was in orbit, and Glenn completed his mission with the space craft under his manual control. As he himself said, "Man has been piped aboard as pilot of the space craft. Now we can get rid of some of the automatic equipment and let man take over."

By this time the United States' manned space flight program had both a goal and a target date. The goal was to land men on the moon and bring them safely back to earth. The target date was 1970. Project Apollo, as the moon project was named, had begun. Russia, too, had determined on the moon as a primary objective, and each country embarked on a program more costly than any the world had yet seen.

Both countries rapidly gained more and more experience in manned space flight. By the end of 1963, four Americans and six Russians formed the still select group of astronauts who had circled the globe. One of them was a woman—the first woman to journey into space. She was Valentina Vladimirovna Tereshkova, who was launched in *Vostok VI* on June 16, 1963, and completed 48 earth orbits.

In the following year the Russians put up the first space craft to carry a team of astronauts: *Voskhod I*, launched on October 12, 1964, carried a three-man crew on its 16-orbit flight. In 1965 came the first space walks: in March the Russian Alexei Leonev became the first man to step out into space from an orbiting space craft; less than three months later Edward H. White "walked" in space outside the American *Gemini 4*. The next year, 1966, saw the first dual launch and docking, or link-up, in space when the crew of *Gemini 8* successfully docked their capsule with an orbiting unmanned Agena target vehicle.

By this time a craft from earth had already made a soft landing on the moon. The Russian *Luna IX* had touched down on the moon in January 1966 and had for three days sent close-up photographs of its surface back to earth. In June of the same year the American *Surveyor 1* also landed and sent back television pictures. Two years later the first unmanned craft went around the moon and returned to earth—the Russian *Zond V*, in September 1968.

The first men to see the far side of the moon were three Americans, the crew of *Apollo 8*, who went into lunar orbit on Christmas Eve, 1968. Their commander, Frank Borman, commented from orbit that the moon seemed "not a very exciting place to live or work." But that men will live and work there seems certain. The year 1969 sees their first attempt at landing. And afterwards? Already Mars and Venus beckon as the next staging-points of men's journey into space.

Man has begun to explore earth's neighbors in the solar system; one day, perhaps, he may reach out even farther into the galaxy, toward the distant stars.

An early automobile — the Phebus Aster *of 1900.*

Glossary

In this Glossary, as in the rest of the book, the symbol ☞ means that the term it follows has its own alphabetical entry in the Glossary, to which you may refer for a fuller definition or for more information.

AERODYNAMICS That part of the mechanics of fluids that deals with the dynamics of gases. Particularly the study of forces acting on bodies moving in air. '

AILERONS Hinged or pivoted flaps fixed on the trailing edge of an airplane's wing. They enable the pilot to control the roll of the airframe and to effect such maneuvers as banks.

AIRCRAFT Any flying machine supported by the dynamic action of air on its surfaces or by buoyancy. Heavier-than-air craft, such as airplanes☞, helicopters☞, and gliders, are called *aerodynes*. Lighter-than-air craft, such as balloons☞ and airships☞, are called *aerostats*.

AIR-CUSHION VEHICLE See HOVERCRAFT.

AIR NAVIGATION The process of directing the movement of air traffic from one point to another. Formerly, the principal method was pilotage, performed by noting various landmarks passed and comparing them with information given on the aeronautical chart. Today, electronic aids—such as radio and radar☞—are widely employed.

AIRPLANE An aircraft☞ propelled by an engine and supported by the upward thrust of the air on its fixed wings.

AIRPORT A tract of land with facilities for the landing, takeoff, shelter, supply, and repair of aircraft☞, especially one used for regular passenger traffic.

AIRSHIP A propelled and steered aerial balloon☞ dependent on gases for flotation. The largest airship ever built was the German *Hindenburg*, with a length of 803 feet. Airships were used to great effect in World War I for patrolling, submarine☞ hunting, and as escorts for ships. Since they can carry great loads and operate in adverse weather conditions, they make excellent communications relay stations.

AMPHIBIOUS VEHICLES Vehicles designed to operate both on land and in water; a seaplane☞ is amphibious if it is equipped with a retractable

Comet 4B *airliner*

Washington airport control tower

Airship of the U.S. Navy

Amphibious automobile

Automobiles on the production line

Modern sporting balloon

wheel landing gear. Amphibious vehicles were widely used for landing operations and in coastal defense during World War II. The DUKW ("duck"), first used in World War II, is a boat and a 2½-ton truck☞ equipped with high-flotation tires that can be inflated or deflated by the driver.

ATOMIC ENERGY (also called "nuclear energy") The energy released when the particles making up the nucleus of an atom are rearranged, whether by fission of a heavy nucleus or by fusion of light nuclei into heavier ones.

AUTOGIRO A rotorcraft☞ with a freely rotating rotor; the rotor is not powered, and the craft cannot hover or rise vertically. It is driven forward by a propeller☞. The principle of the autogiro is used in the helicopter☞ (which has a powered rotor), and also in such convertiplanes as the American McDonnell XV-1 and the British Fairey Rotodyne. In these, the rotor is powered for vertical takeoff and landing☞ by jets at the blade tips.

AUTOMATIC PILOT (also called "autopilot") An automatic system for steering an aircraft☞ or other vehicle. It replaces the human pilot in guided missiles, and in ordinary aircraft may be used to relieve the pilot, to make automatic approaches to landing fields, and to control rapid maneuvers (such as tracking a dodging target). Also used to steer ships, submarines☞, torpedoes, and spacecraft☞.

AUTOMOBILE A self-propelled vehicle designed for road travel, especially for passengers. Automobiles are usually powered by an internal-combustion engine☞, but may also be powered by electricity, or even by turbojet engines. The first automobiles were powered by steam.

BALLISTICS The science concerned with the laws governing the motion of projectiles☞.

BALLOON A container for gas that is lighter than air, designed to rise and float in the atmosphere. To this gasbag may be attached a payload consisting of scientific instruments, or a car to carry passengers.

BICYCLE A vehicle with two wheels in tandem, a seat, handlebars for steering, and pedals by which it is propelled. Bicycling is one of the cheapest forms of transportation.

BOXCAR A roofed freight car used in railroad☞ transportation.

BRIDGE A structure specifically erected to span a natural or artificial obstacle, such as a river or a railroad. Usually, bridges support a footpath or roadway for pedestrians, a highway, or a railroad. They may be movable (like a drawbridge or swing bridge), or fixed.

BULKHEAD (1) A partition that divides a ship into watertight compartments to reduce the extent of seawater flooding in case of damage, and also to strengthen the hull structure. (2) A reinforcing frame or partition in the body of an airplane☞.

BUS (short for "omnibus") A wheeled, trackless, self-propelled passenger vehicle. There are many types of buses, designed to carry as few as 9 or as many as 50 people.

CONTAINER TRANSPORTATION (also called "containerization"). A system of land-sea transportation in which freight is carried in sealed containers of standard dimensions, designed to fit into foreign and domestic railroad freight cars, trucks☞, cargo ships, and airplanes☞. Transportation by containers, developed in the United States during and after World War II, can make cargo handling considerably cheaper, although special ships must be built, or cargo liners☞ converted, before it can be exploited to the full. One of its chief advantages is the speeding of delivery: a 1966 experiment showed that containerization could cut the transit time between Chicago and Birmingham, England, from 19 days to 14 days. Since 1966, American companies have joined hands with British and other European organizations to operate container services; and several countries have schemes in hand for developing special container ports. Such ports would include fully automated storage areas, and would be equipped with modern handling facilities: lift-on, lift-off

The Draisienne *bicycle (1818)*

Harbor bridge for boat trains

Loading a container into a jet

A horse-drawn London omnibus of 1860

A petrol-driven London omnibus of 1919

Electrically driven trolley cars—in retirement at a museum

trucks☞ that load and discharge containers with their own gear, and large cranes for handling the heaviest containers.

CONVEYER A continually moving, materials-handling machine that transports its load or cargo over a fixed path.

DIESEL ENGINE An internal-combustion engine☞ in which air is compressed to a temperature that is sufficiently high to ignite fuel injected directly into the cylinder. The combustion operates a piston. See also LOCOMOTIVE.

DOCK (1) An enclosure or a waterway between piers or wharves, for the reception of ships (see also DRY DOCK). (2) A platform for loading and unloading trucks☞, railroad freight cars, etc. (3) An airplane☞ hangar or repair shed.

DRY DOCK A dock☞ from which water has been drained and then excluded—usually by means of gates or hollow floating boxes called *caissons*—so that the lower part of a ship may be inspected or repaired.

FUSELAGE The part of an airplane's structure to which the main wings are attached; it accommodates the pilot, passengers, cargo, and so on.

HARBOR Any body of water sufficiently deep for ships to enter and shelter from storms or other natural hazards. A modern harbor is both a terminal for incoming and outgoing ships and a place where ships are built, launched, and repaired. Most harbors are situated at the mouths of rivers or at some point where cargoes may be transferred easily inland—by river barges, by railroad☞, or in trucks☞.

HELICOPTER A rotorcraft☞ that derives its support in the air solely from the reaction of a stream of air driven downward by propellers☞ revolving around vertical axes. It is the most successful vertical takeoff and landing☞ aircraft so far developed.

HELIPORT Any place used for the landing and takeoff of helicopters☞, from the roof of a city building to the platform of an oil rig at sea.

Unloading an aircraft by conveyor

Rooftop heliport in central New York

Cross-Channel Hovercraft

Experimental ocean hydrofoil

The Russian atomic icebreaker Lenin

HOVERCRAFT (also called "air-cushion vehicle") A vehicle that rides on a cushion of air created by a lifting propeller☞ or ducted fan—usually rising a few inches or a few feet above the surface it travels over. That surface may be firm land, mud, marsh, or water.

HULL (1) The frame of a ship (excluding masts, sails, and rigging). (2) The framework of a rigid airship☞, which encloses the gasbag and supports the car. (3) The armored body of a vehicle such as a tank.

HYDROFOILS Underwater plates or fins attached to a seaplane☞ boat or ship that act as wings and lift the hull☞ clear of the water as the vehicle gains speed.

HYDROPLANE A speedboat equipped with hydro-foils☞. Hydroplanes were used as motor gunboats, motor torpedo boats, and air-sea rescue launches during World War II. Faster and more maneuverable than hovercraft☞, they are especially popular as racing vehicles on lakes, rivers, and reservoirs.

HYPERSONIC FLIGHT Flight carried out at a speed five or more times the speed of sound. See also SUPERSONIC FLIGHT.

ICEBREAKERS Ships designed to clear a channel through ice, propelled usually by diesel-electric—but sometimes by atomic—power. Their design includes a reinforced hull☞, often steel-plated, to resist crushing, and a rudder enabling the vessel to back off and charge the ice. A large fuel capacity is essential, and this need led to the development of the world's first atomic icebreaker, the Russian *Lenin* (launched in 1957).

INTERNAL-COMBUSTION ENGINE A heat engine in which the pressure necessary to move the mechanism is produced by the ignition or burning of a fuel-air mixture within the cylinder.

JET PROPULSION The propulsion of a body by means of force resulting from the rearward discharge of a *jet* (a high-speed stream of fluid) through a nozzle or orifice. The forces responsible for the propulsion are usually exerted

85

against the inside of the forward part of the body. A simple example of jet propulsion is the motion given to an inflated toy balloon when the compressed air is allowed to escape.

JUMBO JET The popular name for a large subsonic jet airliner seating nearly 500 passengers, especially for the Boeing 747.

LAUNCHING PAD The platform and supporting facilities required for the erection and launching of a ground-based, rocket-propelled vehicle.

LINER Any ship maintaining a regular service for the transportation of passengers or cargo.

LOCOMOTIVE A self-propelled vehicle used for moving trains on railroads. Steam locomotives produce steam by heating water in a boiler (see STEAM ENGINE), and carry their own supplies of fuel and water with them. Electric locomotives obtain their power either from overhead wires, or from a third rail by means of a sliding contact device called a *shoe*. Diesel locomotives generate their own power (see DIESEL ENGINE), which is more economical than electricity and more powerful than steam. Most modern locomotives are driven by diesel power, which enables them to stop and start instantly, and to make long runs without refueling or servicing.

MERCHANT SHIPS Vessels used for commercial carrying on the oceans and on large bodies of inland water, such as the Great Lakes in North America. The main classes of merchant-ship transportation today include general cargo, bulk dry or liquid cargo, and passenger. Transportation by sea is slower than transportation by rail, truck☞, or air, but its cost per ton-mile is usually far lower.

MOTOR CAR (1) An automobile☞. (2) A passenger car, equipped with its own motor, for use on electrified railroads. Trailer cars are often attached to make up a multiple-unit train.

MOTORCYCLE A wheeled, trackless, self-propelled vehicle for land transportation, with two or three wheels, and sometimes an attached sidecar for passengers.

The Flying Scotsman

Motorcycle racing

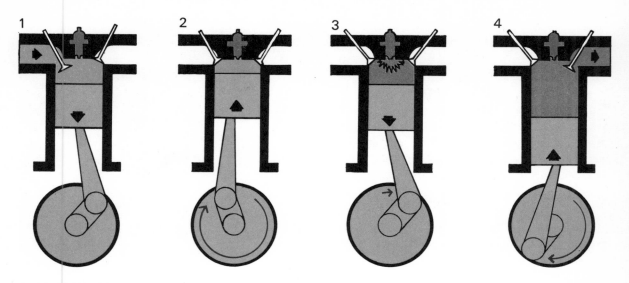

Internal-combustion Engines   *The diesel engine works by means of a set pattern of piston strokes (above). First, the piston draws in air. Second, it compresses it. Third, injected fuel ignites and exploding gases force the piston down. Fourth, the piston expels used gases. The diesel engine has at least seven moving parts; but an ingenious new type, the Wankel, has only one—a 3-lobed rotor turning on a central gear (below). Inlet and exhaust ports in the casing are opened and closed by the lobes of the rotor as it revolves.*

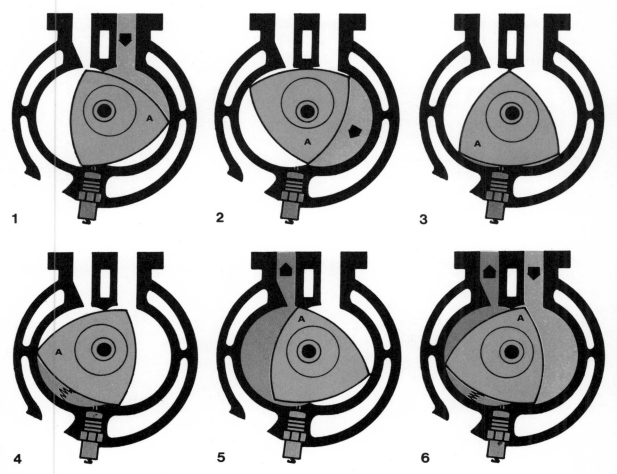

MOTOR SCOOTER A low, self-propelled vehicle, usually two-wheeled. Smaller and less powerful than the motorcycle☞, and designed so that the rider does not straddle the engine.

MOTOR SHIPS Merchant ships☞, including passenger ships, cargo ships, and tankers☞, that are propelled by diesel☞ or other internal-combustion engines☞. The first ocean-going motor ship was the cargo liner *Selandia,* which was fitted with diesel engines in 1912.

NAVIGATION The science of ascertaining the position of a ship and of directing its course by observation and calculation.

NAVIGATION INSTRUMENTS Measuring devices in ships and aircraft☞ for determining geographic position. The most revolutionary of these have been the magnetic compass, the sextant, the gyrocompass, radio, and radar☞.

NOSE CONE The protective cone at the forward end of a missile or space vehicle containing the instruments, and necessary to withstand the operational conditions of launching and flight, as well as the conditions encountered on re-entering the earth's atmosphere.

NUCLEAR ENERGY See ATOMIC ENERGY.

PRECISION APPROACH RADAR (PAR) A radar☞ system established on an aïrfield for observation of an aircraft's position with regard to an approach path for landing; it is especially intended to provide an aircraft with guidance during its approach.

PROJECTILE Any body projected or thrown, such as a shell, rocket☞, or guided missile.

PROPELLER A power-driven screw producing a thrust by reason of its rotation in the air (for airplanes☞) or in the sea (for ships). In airplanes the propellers are usually mounted directly on the engine drive shaft in front of or behind the engine housing; in ships, they are usually fitted as low as possible at the stern. High-speed aircraft need means for changing the blade angle during flight.

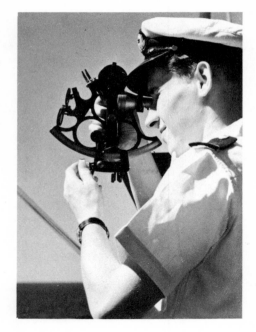

Using a sextant in marine navigation

Thunderbird *missile on transporter*

Water flow around a propeller

Radar scanner on an ocean liner

Railroad junction

The Russian satellite Sputnik I

RADAR A radio detecting device that emits and focuses a powerful scanning beam of ultra-high-frequency waves and establishes, through the reception and timing of reflected waves, the distance, altitude, and direction of motion of any object in the path of its beam.

RAILROAD A system of transportation in which trains of cars, drawn by one power unit—usually a diesel or electric locomotive☞—run upon tracks of steel rails. Today, railroad service to the public is in three main sectors: transportation of passengers, freight (petroleum, coal, machinery, livestock, etc), and mails. As highways and highway freight services have improved, railroad mileage has been decreasing in Britain and in the United States—but railroads are improving their efficiency and their capacity for freight.

ROCKET A general term for a wide variety of jet-propelled missiles, including research vehicles, thrust devices, and even fireworks. A rocket's forward motion results from reaction to a rearward high-speed flow of hot gases generated by combustion. Both solid and liquid propellants are used to provide combustion gases.

ROCKET STAGING A means of minimizing the weight of large missiles or space vehicles by the use of multiple stages. The first stage, usually the biggest, is called the *booster*; the next stages—successively smaller—are called *sustainers*. Each stage is a vehicle in itself, carrying its own propellant and its own control system. Once the propellant of a given stage is expended, the dead weight of that stage—including rocket engine and controls—can be dropped. This means that the mass that remains to be accelerated becomes lighter, and makes it possible to achieve far greater range, speed, and altitude.

ROTORCRAFT A type of aircraft☞ that is supported in flight by rotating blades or wings—for example, a helicopter☞ or an autogiro☞.

SAILING SHIPS All large, sea-going craft propelled by the action of wind on a sail.

SATELLITES, ARTIFICIAL Man-made objects or vehicles intended to orbit the earth, the moon, or a planet. The first two successful man-made satellites—*Sputnik I* and *Sputnik II*—were launched by the Russians in October and November 1957 respectively; *Sputnik II* carried a live dog on board. The third successful man-made satellite was the United States' *Explorer I*—launched in October 1959. The first satellite to carry a man (Y. A. Gagarin) successfully into space was *Vostok I* (on April 12, 1961). This Russian satellite completed slightly more than one orbit before returning to earth.

SEAPLANE   An airplane☞ designed for use over the sea, especially one fitted with floats to support it on water.

SNORKEL   An extended pipe, used in submarines☞, to suck in outside air, thus enabling the craft to run submerged and to charge batteries while doing so. It makes the detection of submarines by radar very difficult, particularly in a rough sea.

SPACE CARRIERS   Rocket-powered vehicles used to launch spacecraft☞ beyond the earth's atmosphere. Their development became possible only after atmospheric sounding and ballistic-missile technology had become highly reliable, and after launching and handling techniques had been perfected. The firing of the first small space carriers took place in the late 1950s.

SPACECRAFT   A manned vehicle designed to operate in space, outside the earth's atmosphere.

SPACE PROBES   Vehicles designed to collect information on outer space, and on the bodies found in outer space.

SPACE STATION   A laboratory in space where scientific and exploratory work can be carried out. The first elementary space stations, in the form of artificial satellites☞, were placed in orbit around the earth in the International Geophysical Year (July 1957-December 1958). The problem now remains to place a manned station in space. Such a station would have to protect its occupants against environmental hazards such as high-energy radiation and meteor collision. Its design would also have to

Model of an imagined "spaceliner"

Fanciful model for a space station

Space Rockets *Pictured here are the Russian* Vostok (*right*), *and the U.S.* Ranger (*top*) *and* Saturn i.

ensure—among other things—that the atmosphere in the cabin could sustain life, and that the temperature remained within acceptable limits. Another major problem is weightlessness.

STEAM ENGINE An engine in which the expansive action of steam generated in a boiler moves a sliding piston in a cylinder. Steam engines are still the most common type of propulsion for big ships, although the diesel engine☞ has been gaining wide acceptance in some countries for ships of medium tonnage☞. On railroads☞, steam engines have been largely replaced by diesel engines and electric power.

STEAMSHIPS Strictly speaking, the term refers only to large, seagoing craft propelled by the power of steam—but the word is commonly used to describe any commercial powered vessel.

STREETCAR A public passenger vehicle running regularly along a fixed route, usually on rails. Electric streetcars first operated in 1888.

SUBMARINE A ship that can be submerged and navigated under water. The fastest submerged Atlantic crossing (6 days 11 hours 55 mins) was made in August 1958 by the U.S. nuclear-powered submarine *Nautilus*.

SUPERSONIC FLIGHT Flight at a speed in excess of the speed of sound. Flights at a speed more than five times the speed of sound enter the hypersonic speed range.

SWEPT-BACK WINGS (also called "swept wings") Airplane wings slanted so that the outer portion of the wing is downstream from the inner portion. Introduced in the late 1940s, they helped to solve the problems of buffeting and loss of stability that occur as the speed of an aircraft approaches the speed of sound.

SWING-WING AIRCRAFT (also called "variable geometry aircraft") Aircraft☞ with movable wings that can be swung back for supersonic flight☞ and opened for landing.

TAIL UNIT The rear portion of an airplane☞, including the elevator, fin, and rudder.

The U.S. nuclear submarine Nautilus

Experimental swing-wing aircraft

Tail unit of Swingtail 44

Caterpillar CAT D4 *bulldozer*

London subway tunnel

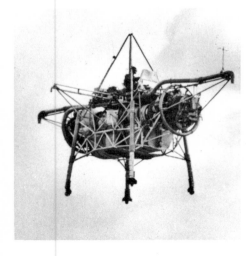

Experimental VTOL aircraft of 1953

TANKERS A class of vessels constructed for the transportation of liquid bulk cargo, especially crude petroleum.

TENDER (1) A floating and mobile repair and supply station for ships. (2) The car attached to a steam locomotive☞ to carry its supplies of fuel and water.

TONNAGE A measurement of the size or capacity of a ship, which may be calculated in several different ways. *Gross* tonnage is a measure of a merchant ship's capacity, the "ton" in this case being 100 cubic feet. *Deadweight* tonnage is the total weight of cargo carried. *Displacement* tonnage, a term used chiefly of warships, is the amount of water displaced by a ship.

TRACKED VEHICLES Vehicles with wheels running on a track that lays itself as it goes. Its purpose is to provide the wheels with a firm surface on uneven or soft ground.

TRACTOR A wheeled, self-propelled vehicle used to haul other vehicles or equipment and to operate towed implements.

TRUCK A wheeled, trackless, self-propelled vehicle used for the transportation of commodities overland.

TUNNEL A structure designed to provide a passageway (usually under the ground) under an obstruction such as a road or a river. Several proposals for long-distance tube tunnels have been put forward in recent years. In 1966 Britain and France agreed on the construction of a *Channel Tunnel* that could speed transportation between Britain and the Continent while greatly cutting its cost. The tunnel would consist of twin railroad tunnels capable of carrying electric passenger trains, freight trains, and road vehicles. It would travel under sea for 23 of its 32 miles.

VERTICAL TAKEOFF AND LANDING (VTOL) CRAFT Aircraft☞ that take off and land without a run. Such aircraft have the advantage of being able to operate from small airports☞ or from small clearings in wooded terrain. The most successful VTOL craft to date is the helicopter☞.

Index

Picture Credits

43 (T) P & O Steam Navigation Company
(C) A Shell photograph
(B) Photo Babcock & Wilcox (Operations) Limited, London
45 Mansell Collection
46 © 1969, Walt Disney Productions
47 U.S. Navy photo
49 Photo British Hovercraft Corporation
50 Mansell Collection
53 (C) Mansell Collection
(B) Photo Science Museum, London
57 (TR) Photo Société National de Construction Aeronautique du Nord, Paris
(2nd R) Imperial War Museum, London
(3rd R) British Aircraft Corporation, Weybridge Division
(BR) Boeing Aircraft Company, London
61 Photo courtesy Hawker Siddeley Aviation
62 British Crown Copyright. Science Museum, London
63 Photo *The Sunday Times Magazine*
65 (T) Radio Times Hulton Picture Library
(C) Photo Westland Aircraft Company, Yeovil
(B) Photo James Pickerell
67 (T) Royal Aircraft Establishment, Farnborough
(C) Boeing Aircraft Company, London
(B) By permission of British Aircraft Corporation Limited
71 (R) NASA
73 Grumman Aircraft Engineering Corporation
75 NASA Photo
77 Photo from the Mount Wilson and Palomar Observatories
78 Montague Motor Museum
80 (T) Hawker Siddeley Aviation Limited
(C) Courtesy United States Information Service
(B) Aero Service Corporation
81 (T) Keystone
(C) Aldus Archives

(B) Picturepoint, London
82 (C) Barnaby's Picture Library
(B) Official U.S. Air Force Photo
83 (T) Mary Evans Picture Library
(CL) Museum of British Transport
(CR) Picturepoint, London
(B) Photo R. G. S. Woodburn
84 (T) Courtesy United States Information Service
(B) Courtesy of Pan American World Airways
85 (T) Barnaby's Picture Library
(C) By courtesy of Fox Photos Ltd.
(B) Novosti Press Agency
86 (C) Barnaby's Picture Library
(B) Photo Harry Stanfield

87 (B) after Donald H. Marter, *Engines*, Thames & Hudson Ltd., London, 1965
88 (T) Photo J. Allan Cash
(C) British Crown Copyright. Supplied by Central Office of Information
(B) British Crown Copyright. National Physical Laboratory
89 (T) Photo J. Allan Cash
(C) By courtesy of Fox Photos Ltd.
(B) Novosti Press Agency
90 (T) (B) Stills from the MGM Presentation of Stanley Kubrick's Production of *2001: A Space Odyssey*
91 (R) Novosti Press Agency
(TL, BL) NASA Photos
92 (T) Official U.S. Navy Photo
(C) (B) Courtesy United States Information Service
93 (T) Aldus Archives
(C) Photo London Transport
(B) Courtesy Rolls-Royce Limited
Rudolph Britto 71(R)
Gordon Cramp 15(BL)
David Litchfield 18, 19
Edward Poulton 53(T)
John Tyler 8, 15(T), 39, 48, 55, 57(L), 58, 59, 68, 71(L)(C), 87
Peter Warner 21(T), 36

Endpapers: George Stephenson's Rocket *wins the Rainhill Trials, October 1829.*